Being a College Counselor
on Today's Campus

Being a College Counselor on Today's Campus

Roles, Contributions, and Special Challenges

BRUCE S. SHARKIN

Routledge
Taylor & Francis Group
New York   London

Routledge
Taylor & Francis Group
711 Third Avenue
New York, NY 10017

Routledge
Taylor & Francis Group
27 Church Road
Hove, East Sussex BN3 2FA

International Standard Book Number: 978-0-415-88214-9 (Paperback)

Library of Congress Cataloging-in-Publication Data

Sharkin, Bruce S.
    Being a college counselor on today's campus : roles, contributions, and special challenges / Bruce S Sharkin.
        p. cm.
    Includes bibliographical references and index.
    ISBN 978-0-415-88214-9 (pbk.)
    1. Counseling in higher education. 2. Student counselors. I. Title.

LB2343.S488 2011
378.1'9--dc23   2011022957

Visit the Taylor & Francis Web site at
http://www.taylorandfrancis.com

and the Routledge Web site at
http://www.routledgementalhealth.com

In memory of Evan Phillips (1984–2010)
If the measure of one's life is not in how many years
lived but in how many other lives are enriched,
this young man's life was a remarkable one.

Contents

Preface

When you have worked in a professional field for over two decades, as I have, you see the many changes that contributed to the field's evolving over time. I have served as a college counselor my entire professional career. My first true sense of what it means to be a college counselor was in 1988 when I was a predoctoral intern in the counseling center at the University of Florida. In 1989, I was hired to work in the counseling center at Lehigh University in Bethlehem, Pennsylvania. I worked at Lehigh until 2001, when I accepted a similar position at Kutztown University in Kutztown, Pennsylvania, which I continue to hold today. The notable difference, however, is that at Kutztown, counseling center staff members also have faculty status. At Lehigh, like most counseling center staff members, I was considered professional staff and also held (and continue to hold) adjunct faculty status with the Counseling and Human Services graduate program.

The positions I held at Lehigh and now hold at Kutztown afford me an interesting vantage point, as I have worked as a college counselor in different capacities, one more traditional and one with faculty rank and rights. Working in these two institutions also has given me experience within two very divergent campus cultures: Lehigh is a private institution with a student population that is mostly economically privileged, whereas Kutztown is a state institution with a student body that is characterized by more working-class-background and first-generation college students. The differences in working with these two contrasting student populations are sometimes quite striking, for example, in terms of available resources if off-campus services are needed (much greater for Lehigh than Kutztown students) and the need for students to work while in school (much higher percentage of Kutztown students than Lehigh students).

In addition to having worked as a college counselor in two different types of institutions with contrasting student populations, I have also served in a multitude of capacities and engaged in a variety of activities in my role as a college counselor. This is the case for most, if not all, college counselors. Since first entering the field, I have served as coordinator and cocoordinator of a peer education program, outreach coordinator, and chair and administrative director of counseling services. I have also presented countless outreach programs, taught numerous graduate courses on various counseling subjects, published research articles and a previous book (*College Students in Distress: A Resource Guide for Faculty, Staff, and Campus Community*), presented at professional conferences, served as an editorial board member for professional counseling journals, served on doctoral dissertation committees, served on a variety of university and faculty committees, participated in various capacities in professional associations, supervised dozens of graduate student trainees, provided after-hours on call emergency services, and been involved in establishing, reviewing, and revising campus policies regarding student mental health.

My intent in sharing my professional background and experiences is simply to show that I am in a good position to write a book about the many dimensions and challenges involved in the profession of college counseling and to be able to describe what college counseling is, how it became what it is today, and where it might be headed in the future.

There has been increasing attention in recent years, both positive and negative, on college student mental health and the provision of counseling services on campuses. Much of this attention has helped to clarify and delineate who we are as college counselors and the many roles we play in the lives of students. However, in my opinion, there continue to be misunderstandings and misperceptions of college counselors, both within and outside of the confines of the colleges themselves. Other college counselors have expressed similar opinions (e.g., Much, Wagener, & Hellenbrand, 2010). Hence, this book is designed to provide a thorough picture of the college counselor on today's campus.

Returning to the idea of how much change has occurred in the profession since I first began my career, this book will be devoted, in part, to an examination of the factors contributing to such change and how college counseling has evolved since its early days. When I reflected on some of the events and issues just in the past two decades, I thought of the following:

- new technology makes electronic devices such as cell phones and laptop computers common in everyday use;
- it is more typical for students to remain in college for more than four years;
- there is a perception that college students are more emotionally troubled than in years past;
- competition for entry into college has intensified;
- there is much more diversity in the student population, which brings a richness to campus life but also poses challenges in terms of meeting varied and unique needs of different student groups, as well as the potential for tensions to emerge when intolerance of differences is experienced;
- more economically disadvantaged students can now attend college;
- in general, more students are able to attend college today that could not in the past, particularly because of enactment of the Americans With Disabilities Act (ADA) of 1990, which extends legal protection from discrimination to individuals with emotional and psychological disorders;
- the use of psychotropic medication for young people has become fairly commonplace;
- new anxieties and fears exist following the September 11th terrorist attacks;
- there is the perception that campuses are less safe than they once were following the mass murder at Virginia Tech and other high-profile cases of campus violence and crime;

- there has been an increase in lawsuits, many of which garnered media attention following student suicides, homicides,
  and ADA violations;
- sensationalistic tales of campus life and culture, such as those
  presented in the book *Binge: What Your College Student Won't
  Tell You* (Seaman, 2005), paint a portrait of college life filled
  with widespread alcohol and drug use, casual sexual encounters, class and racial tensions, and other problems. Even
  scholarly publications seemed to exploit the perceived epi-
  demic of college student crises with titles such as *College of the
  Overwhelmed: The Campus Mental Health Crisis and What to
  Do About It* (Kadison & DiGeronimo, 2004).

I imagine that there are other issues or events that have shaped
the evolution of college counseling in the past two decades that I
neglected to include here. The important point is that much has taken
place in the years that I have been working in this profession, and it
has been enlightening to observe and be a part of this evolution. My
goal is to translate these experiences and observations into a meaningful book that will explore the many facets and complexities of the
work of college counselors and demonstrate why college counseling is
now clearly a specialty field within counseling.

Although this book is designed to be of particular interest to practicing college counselors and those considering or pursuing a career
in college counseling, I believe this book will also be of interest to
graduate students who seek training experiences in college counseling
centers as well as those already placed at counseling center practicum
or internship sites. In addition, this book can be a valuable resource
for college administrators and student services personnel who continue to advocate for and work with mental health professionals on
their campuses.

Acknowledgments

I wish to express my gratitude to Bill Chabala, Nick Ladany, and Julie Perone for their thoughtful input and suggestions on my proposal for this book and to Aimee Adams, Bill Hopkins, Brian Van Brunt, and Julie Perone for their valuable comments and suggestions on earlier drafts of the book manuscript. I also want to express my appreciation to Carolyn Brady and Amy Lenhart for their insight and suggestions regarding special issues for counselors who work in community college settings. In addition, I am grateful to several people who provided encouragement and support as I completed the many hours of research and writing that went into this book. In particular, I wish to acknowledge Lisa Ruff, Roger and Marie Phillips, Nick Ladany, Lisa Coulter, Aimee Adams, Vivian Davis-Martinez, Paul Quinn, Deborah Bevvino, Caitlin Bevvino-Ring, Sherry Abelove, Bill Hopkins, Keith Sharkin, Michelle Sharkin, Tyler Sharkin, Conrad Sharkin, and Nikki Sharkin. I need to extend a special note of love and appreciation to K. K. Sharkin, who always waited so patiently as I typed away at my computer.

About the Author

Bruce S. Sharkin received his PhD in counseling psychology from the University of Maryland in 1989. Dr. Sharkin is a staff psychologist and associate professor in the Department of Counseling and Psychological Services at Kutztown University in Kutztown, Pennsylvania. He has over 20 years of experience in college counseling and currently serves as administrative director and chair of his department. Dr. Sharkin is the author or coauthor of over 25 journal articles and a previous book titled *College Students in Distress: A Resource Guide for Faculty, Staff, and Campus Community*, published in 2006. He has served as an editorial reviewer for the *Journal of College Counseling, Journal of Counseling Psychology,* and *Journal of Counseling and Development*. Dr. Sharkin is currently an editorial advisory board member for the American Counseling Association Publications office.

1

THE SPECIALTY FIELD OF COLLEGE COUNSELING

As a profession, college counseling has been around for many years, yet its emergence as a true specialty seems to have occurred in more recent years. College counseling is now considered a specialty field within the larger professional domain of counseling, similar to long-existing specialties such as addictions counseling and family counseling. This means that it is a field that requires specific qualifications and skills and consists of its own unique experiences and challenges. It also means that being a college counselor encompasses its own sense of professional identity regardless of the particular background or educational credentials of the individual practitioner. Simply stated, there is nothing quite like the experience of being a counselor on a college or university campus. Grayson and Meilman (2006) referred to college counseling as "a world unto itself" (p. 1). The delineation of the unique dimensions of college counseling is the primary mission of this book.

In addition to providing counseling, most college counselors engage in a variety of other tasks. This includes consultation and outreach, supervision and training, research, teaching, and myriad other important contributions to the overall mission of their universities. College counselors may be appreciated and valued in some respects, while at the same time they may be underappreciated and undervalued in other respects. For example, faculty and staff members on a campus are relieved to be able to refer emotionally distressed students to those with more expertise in handling such matters. After all, this is what campus counselors are primarily there for, at least in the eyes of others on campus. But when it comes to the many other roles, responsibilities, and professional activities that college counselors engage in, this is where there may be less acknowledgment of their value.

This chapter will first provide some brief but significant historical perspective on the profession and how it has evolved, particularly over the past 20 to 30 years. This will include some discussion of the tragedy that occurred at Virginia Tech in 2007, for this is an event that significantly changed campus life in general and the role of college counselors in particular. The historical review will be followed by a discussion of the professionals who currently work as college counselors and what skills are needed to be an effective college counselor on today's campus.

The Evolution of College Counseling

Historical Roots

The early beginnings of what is now called college counseling have been written about and summarized by others (Dean & Meadows, 1995; Hodges, 2001; Meadows, 2000; Prescott, 2008). Prescott's review is perhaps the most thorough and interesting to read, though she is not a college counselor and rather writes from the perspective of a historian. According to Prescott (2008), mental health services first appeared at American colleges and universities during the 1920s in an effort to broaden health services in higher education after the First World War. In those days, such services were generally referred to as mental hygiene programs. Prescott noted that there were only a dozen or so private colleges that instituted these programs during the 1920s and 1930s, with Princeton being the first.

Based on the description of what these services entailed, it seems that they were primarily the domain of psychiatry, and not surprisingly there was a strong sense of social stigma associated with utilizing them back then. The sense of stigma was certainly not helped by the prevailing sentiments of homophobia, anti-Semitism, and oppression of women that influenced these early efforts at treating mental illness on campus (Prescott, 2008). Prescott described how there were also strong feelings of opposition from faculty members who viewed mental hygiene programs as a form of "coddling" academically underperforming students. Indeed, there are still some remnants of this attitude that persist today.

Following the Second World War, there was further expansion of mental health services in higher education, in large part due to the influx of veterans who were given financial assistance to enroll in colleges and universities. In the 1950s, a significant proportion of counseling provided was in the form of career counseling to veterans, and the vocational planning for these veterans opened up avenues of exploration into personal and social concerns (Hodges, 2001). Theories of late-adolescent development that emerged at the time also helped focus attention on the importance of nurturing the emotional maturation process of college students, further expanding the role of counseling into more personal and social dimensions of students' lives.

The 20-year period from 1960 to 1980 has been characterized as perhaps the most significant period of growth in the development of the profession of college counseling (Meadows, 2000). Many counseling centers assumed increasing responsibility for testing services, including national testing programs such as the Scholastic Aptitude Test and Graduate Record Exam (Weissberg, 1987). Early pioneers such as Thomas Magoon, Charles Warnath, and Allen Ivey made significant contributions through research and publications to a young but blossoming field. Common standards were adopted by the International Association of Counseling Services to govern the accreditation of counseling services at different types of institutions of higher education. Despite the tremendous strides that were being made, Meadows related how this period represented a serious challenge to the development of the profession as well. Particularly during the 1970s, the field was trying to advance while facing the threat of looming cuts during difficult economic times, something that the field is once again experiencing today.

The 1980s Through the 2000s: Growing Concern
About College Student Mental Health

Beginning in the 1980s, research began to emerge showing an increase in the severity of problems being treated in college counseling centers. For example, Robbins, May, and Corazzini (1985) reported that a significant percentage of counseling center staff members held the perception that the severity of problems was on the rise. A similar finding was subsequently reported based on the perceptions of counseling center directors (O'Malley, Wheeler, Murphey, O'Connell, & Waldo, 1990). During the 1980s, the traditional developmental approach of college counseling started to give way to the medical model with an emphasis on assessment and diagnosis of disorders (Hodges, 2001), and counseling centers began to merge more with health services (Cooper, Resnick, Rodolfa, & Douce, 2008). Career counseling, once the predominant domain of college counselors, was increasingly becoming a separate service provided by others on campus (Cooper et al., 2008).

As the decade of the 1990s ushered in, Stone and Archer (1990) argued that the purported trend of increasing numbers of students with serious psychological problems was a key challenge facing counseling centers in the new decade. Their article has been deemed to be crucial for setting the tone for the entire decade of the 1990s (Cooper et al., 2008) and continues to be just as influential in the world of college counseling today. Bishop (1990) wrote a similar article making the same claim, and other articles subsequently appeared addressing concerns such as ethical dilemmas associated with increasing psychopathology among college students (Gilbert, 1992). However, the Stone and Archer article remains one of the most cited in the college counseling literature.

Most college counselors in the field at that time believed that the trend of increasing severity was occurring and did not question what was documented in the Stone and Archer (1990) article. However, a closer review of the studies cited by Stone and Archer revealed a lack of convincing evidence (other than the perceptions of counseling center staff members) to support the purported trend (Sharkin, 1997). An ongoing debate subsequently ensued over whether there was a true trend. If in fact there was an increase in the level of distress of college students over the years, particularly those that came to the attention of college counselors, such a trend was difficult to demonstrate through research (Sharkin & Coulter, 2005).

Several large-scale longitudinal studies were subsequently conducted to test the notion that problems presented in counseling centers were becoming increasingly more severe (Benton, Robertson, Tseng, Newton, & Benton, 2003; Cornish, Kominars, Riva, McIntosh, &

Henderson, 2000; Kettmann, Schoen, Moel, Cochran, Greenberg, & Corkery, 2007; Pledge, Lapan, Heppner, Kivlighan, & Roehlke, 1998; A. J. Schwartz, 2006). These studies varied in the time period assessed (ranging from 6 to 13 years), sample size (ranging from 827 to 13,257), and the measures used (from one to multiple measures, most of which were completed at intake, except in the Benton et al. study). A detailed summary of these studies by Much and Swanson (2010) shows that the purported trend of increasing psychopathology has not yet been demonstrated.

Of all of the studies, it was the Benton et al. (2003) study that garnered the most attention, for it was and continues to be cited as evidence for the trend. Though it was an ambitious and important study, there were frequent misinterpretations of its findings due to its methodological shortcomings (Sharkin, 2004a). Nonetheless, the publication of that one study helped continue to fuel national media coverage of college student mental health concerns that had already begun since the start of the new millennium (Arenson, 2004; Duenwald, 2004; Goode, 2003; K. Kelly, 2001; Kirn, 2003; McGinn & DePasquale, 2004; Shea, 2002; Young, 2003).

The publication of the Benton et al. (2003) study was soon followed by the publication of several books on the subject of college student mental health, including the widely recognized *College of the Overwhelmed: The Campus Mental Health Crisis and What to Do About It* (Kadison & DiGeronimo, 2004) and *College Mental Health Practice* (Grayson & Meilman, 2006). Concerns were being raised about the increasing use of psychotropic medication among young people in general (Kluger, 2003) and college students in particular (Carter & Winseman, 2003; Fromm, 2007; Whitaker, 2007; Young, 2003). High-profile cases of student suicide, such as Elizabeth Shin at Massachusetts Institute of Technology in 2000 and several suicides that occurred at New York University in 2003 and 2004, were creating a media frenzy (Kennedy, 2004) and raising anxieties on campuses nationwide (Arenson, 2004). College counseling centers were being characterized as similar to community mental health clinics (Rudd, 2004). A special section in an issue of the *Journal of College Counseling* (Beamish, 2005) was devoted to the problem of "severe and persistent mental illness on college campuses." The special issue included a reiteration of earlier concerns with the lack of research evidence for the trend of increasing problem severity and methodological limitations in the Benton et al. study (Sharkin & Coulter, 2005).

Concern about the mental health care for college students even prompted the federal government to respond with legislative action aimed at strengthening or increasing student access to mental health services on campuses. There was the Campus Care and Counseling Act (HR 3593, 2003; S 2215, 2004), which was eventually incorporated into the Garrett Lee Smith Memorial Act (HR 4799, 2004; S 2634, 2004) and signed into law by then-president George W. Bush in the fall of 2004. A similar type bill, the Mental Health on Campus Improvement Act (HR 1704, 2009; S 682, 2009), was more recently introduced and has been referred to committees in the House of Representatives and Senate, but no further action has been taken by Congress.

Impact of a Tragedy: The Mass Shootings at Virginia Tech in 2007

The level of concern regarding college student mental health and the need for proper assessment and intervention intensified following the tragedy at Virginia Tech on April 17, 2007, in which 32 people were killed by a student named Seung-Hui Cho. Even though this was not the first case of mass murder on a college campus (Charles Whitman, the Texas Tower sniper, killed 16 and wounded 31 people at the University of Texas in 1966), it came at a time of increased hypervigilance to emotionally troubled students, which raised anxieties to a new level. Anxieties had already been high in the wake of several high-profile cases of student suicide, many of which prompted lawsuits against the institutions where they occurred (Arenson, 2004; Franke, 2004). With the Virginia Tech shootings, however, concerns shifted more in the direction of fears of emotionally disturbed students being dangerous to others. Much has been written about the specific events leading up to the shootings, what actually happened on the day of the shootings, and the aftermath of the tragedy (Flynn & Heitzmann, 2008; Shuchman, 2007).

In the ensuing weeks and months following the tragedy, there was considerable scrutiny on what appeared to be missed signs of the potential dangers posed by Cho. For example, it was revealed that a number of people including campus police officers, professors, and fellow students experienced troubling encounters with him. In an article that was published soon after the shootings, Amada (2007) raised questions as to why Cho was not disciplined by the school for the known instances of misconduct, such as stalking female students. It was further revealed that Cho had been briefly committed to a psychiatric hospital in 2005, but his parents had not been informed about this. In the governor-appointed Virginia Tech Review Panel report (2007), it was noted that the campus counseling center failed to communicate with officials in other campus offices or with Cho's parents because of beliefs about privacy restrictions on such communication. The report also made reference to the fact that Cho received "minimal treatment" at the counseling center, but detailed records of any contacts with the center were missing.

News reports eventually revealed that the missing records had been discovered at the home of the former director of the counseling center, Dr. Richard Miller, who was fired from Virginia Tech in December 2005 (Urbina, 2009). According to the reports, on December 14, 2005 (the day Cho was discharged from the psychiatric hospital), Dr. Miller had received an e-mail message about Cho's temporary detention at the hospital and examples of his troubling behavior, which he then forwarded to counseling center staff members with an "FYI" in case the student was seen in the center. Dr. Miller was unaware that Cho had already been seen earlier that day (Schulte & Jackman, 2009). For some reason, the Virginia Tech Review Panel chose not to interview Dr. Miller, perhaps because he had not worked in the counseling center for more than a year before the shootings.

Records show that Cho had three contacts with the campus counseling center in November and December 2005, two times by telephone and once in person (Schulte & Jackman, 2009). In essence, records of all three contacts showed that he was believed to be depressed, had episodes of anxiety, and was socially isolated. Although it was documented that he engaged in self-destructive behavior, it is unclear what this was referring to. However, he reportedly denied suicidal and homicidal thoughts. In the one face-to-face contact he had, he was described as nonverbal, avoidant of eye contact, and showing no emotion. Because this session was at the end of the fall semester, it ended with the counselor encouraging him to return the following month after the semester break, but he never did.

One particular issue of discrepancy revolves around whether Dr. Miller or members of the counseling center staff were informed that he was court ordered by a judge to undergo involuntary treatment at the campus counseling center after his discharge from the psychiatric hospital in December 2005. It has been reported that when he was discharged, the hospital forwarded records to the counseling center, including a court order for treatment (Shuchman, 2007). However, Schulte and Jackman (2009) reported that the campus counselors maintain that they were never informed of such an order to undergo treatment. Clearly, there was a breakdown in communication in this case.

Questions as to whether the counselors involved in evaluating Cho and the former director of counseling will ultimately be held responsible for failing to take steps to prevent what happened will undoubtedly be answered as a result of a pending lawsuit filed by families of two students who were killed that tragic day (Neil, 2010). These were the only two families that would not agree to a settlement from the state that was offered in 2008. While the tragedy itself has had a significant impact on colleges nationwide, the outcome of this lawsuit is likely to have a tremendous impact as well.

The horror of what occurred at Virginia Tech will be felt on campuses for years to come. The sense of safety that was once felt on college campuses has been shattered, and there is now a sense of hypervigilance to the potential risk of another such tragedy (Flynn & Heitzmann, 2008). In many respects, the Virginia Tech tragedy has changed college campuses in the same way the September 11th terrorist attacks changed the entire nation. In particular, colleges have been establishing threat assessment teams on campus in an effort to prevent such tragedies from occurring again. With the emergence of these teams, college counselors have been assuming a growing role in the domain of threat assessment. Hence, this increasing role will be further examined in terms of membership on campus intervention teams (in Chapter 3) and the swirling controversy related to this new role for college counselors (in Chapter 6).

Summary

The evolution of the profession of college counseling has occurred over the span of over 80 years and been influenced by a variety of people and events and the changing culture in which we live. As with most professions, there have been significant changes over the years in terms of the roles and responsibilities of college counselors. Thus, as the field has evolved so have the required skills needed to function as a college counselor on today's campus. The path to becoming a college counselor and the specific skills needed to be effective as a college counselor will be addressed in the following section.

Becoming a College Counselor

How Does One Become a College Counselor?

The path to becoming a college counselor is not always a direct one. Because there are no college counseling degree programs per se, most of the people who end up working as college counselors come from broad-based training programs in counseling psychology, clinical psychology, counseling and human services, mental health counseling, counselor education, and social work. There are master's programs that may offer a specialization in college counseling, as part of either a broader counseling program or student affairs in a higher education program aimed more at developing administrative skills. Typically these programs offer a number of specialized courses devoted to understanding the needs and issues of college students on today's campus. Programs offering a college counseling specialization may require students to participate in a field placement or to complete an internship in a college counseling center, though this may not necessarily involve counseling clients.

Perhaps the field that shares the longest association with college counseling centers is counseling psychology. College counseling centers have a long tradition of serving as training sites for graduate students in counseling psychology programs (Gallessich & Olmstead, 1987; Neimeyer, Bowman, & Stewart, 2001; Richardson & Massey, 1986) and as a rewarding career option for new counseling psychology professionals (Phelps, 1992). In addition, counseling psychology programs have strong ties with counseling centers based on their shared commitment to clinical, research, and training activities (Guinee & Ness, 2000). Although a large percentage of graduates from academic programs in counseling psychology pursue careers as college counselors, it is by no means the only field that prepares people to work as college counselors.

By the 1990s, the college counseling profession was becoming more diverse in terms of the training backgrounds and professional associations of those in the profession (Dean & Meadows, 1995). In a national survey of college counseling center directors (Gallagher, 2010), the professional identity endorsed was as follows: counseling psychologist (38%), clinical psychologist (24%), professional counselor (19%), social worker (8.5%), and mental health professional (4%). Although psychologists may still represent the majority who serve as college counselors, that has been slowly changing and may continue to expand to other mental health professionals over the coming years.

In addition to the particular program of study one pursues is the issue of the type of degree earned. Most college counselors possess either a doctoral degree (PhD, PsyD, or EdD) or a master's degree (MA, MS, MSW, or MEd). Although counseling centers have traditionally been predominantly staffed by individuals with doctoral degrees (Stone, Vespia, & Kanz, 2000), it appears that the number of college counselors with a master's degree may be growing, especially in smaller counseling centers at schools with fewer than 4,000 students (Vespia, 2007). The issue of whether a doctoral degree is required to work in a particular college counseling center will depend on a number of factors. For example, counseling centers that are accredited by the American Psychological Association as predoctoral internship sites are required to hire doctoral-level professionals to fulfill requirements for the provision of clinical supervision that ultimately will fulfill requirements for licensure as well (Rodolfa & Keilin, 2006).

Even counseling centers that are not accredited internship sites may require new hires to have a doctoral degree because this may still be required of supervisors if the center is a training site for doctoral-level graduate students. Counseling centers at schools where there is a doctoral program in counseling may hire doctoral-level practitioners in order to allow for reciprocal benefits of affiliation (e.g., teaching, research, training, etc.). Some universities may simply have a preference to hire doctoral-level clinicians for their counseling centers, perhaps based on a *perception* that such clinicians are more qualified. There does appear to be an advantage of having a doctoral degree if one aspires to serve as a director of a counseling center: 80% of directors reported having a doctoral degree in the most recent survey of directors conducted by the Association of University and College Counseling Center Directors (Barr, Rando, Krylowicz, & Winfield, 2010) and the International Association of Counseling Services requires directors to have doctorates as part of their accreditation standards (Boyd et al., 2003).

There have been many spirited debates over whether a doctoral degree is truly necessary for one to practice effectively as a college counselor. One would be hard-pressed to make a strong case that those with doctoral degrees generally make better clinicians than those with master's degrees. Licensure is often viewed as a better indicator of one's qualifications and is another important credential that many counseling centers require their counselors to possess, but licensure can be obtained at the master's level (e.g., licensed professional counselor or licensed mental health counselor). Many believe it is the skill set and preparation that is most important as opposed to the degree per se. In the next section, what many consider important skills to have to be prepared to enter the profession of college counseling will be discussed. Before doing so, it is important to note that whether one chooses to pursue a master's degree or persevere to earn a doctoral degree, it is essential that the academic program be fully accredited (Dean & Meadows, 1995; Maples, 2000). For example, programs in counseling that are accredited by the Council for Accreditation of Counseling and Related Educational Programs and programs in counseling psychology accredited by the American Psychological Association are thoroughly evaluated to ensure compliance with high standards and to meet licensure requirements.

What Skills Are Necessary to Be a College Counselor on Today's Campus?

As college counseling has become more and more specialized as a profession, the key to being successfully prepared to work as a college counselor is the acquisition of solid, supervised training experiences in a college counseling center. Though there are certain experiences that can be helpful to acquire at the undergraduate level, such as working in residential life or serving as a peer counselor (Maples, 2000), the opportunity to actually provide counseling to college students requires one to be in a graduate degree program. It is critical for anyone who is considering work in college counseling to acquire at least one yearlong training experience working in a counseling center, though training experiences in other types of settings (e.g., a hospital) can be important to broaden one's knowledge of other mental health service agencies (Hinkelman, 2005). This could be in the form of a practicum, a field placement, or an internship. Simply put, the more experience gained in a counseling center, the better prepared and more attractive to employers someone will be for a college counselor position.

Most of the training programs identified earlier train their students to be "generalists" with respect to clinical skills. This means that they are equipped to provide counseling for a wide range of problems. Although being a generalist can be a desirable skill for college counseling (Williams & Edwardson, 2000), there is often interest in hiring individuals who also possess some special skills or expertise. This expertise may involve having experience working with specific problems, such as eating disorders, mood disorders, trauma, grief, or substance abuse. The expertise could also comprise more advanced knowledge and skills working with specific subgroups of students, such as students of color, international students, military veterans, student athletes, or gay, lesbian, bisexual, transgender, or questioning students.

In addition to being a generalist with some specialized skills, to be an effective college counselor requires one to have a keen understanding of college student development and how to be responsive to the struggles of students in ways that will resonate with them. College students represent a diverse population with many unique subpopulations (Lippincott & Lippincott, 2007), but the larger population of college students as a whole shares some common developmental stages and tasks (Ghetie, 2007; Von Steen, 2000). For traditionally aged students (ages 18–24), this is a phase of life that comprises developmental tasks such as autonomy, individuation, identity, and intimacy (Chickering & Reisser, 1993; Francis, 2009). It is a time of transition from adolescence to emerging adulthood (Arnett, 2000), and with that transition come fears and anxieties of assuming adult responsibilities. It can be an especially daunting time, given that college culture encourages participation in various high-risk behaviors, such as alcohol use and sexual activity as a developmentally based form of experimentation (Dworkin, 2005).

The developmental tasks of this stage of life and the myriad potential roadblocks to their successful completion will prompt many students to seek counseling. Clearly then there is a need for college counselors to be well versed in the developmental struggles of traditional college students and how best to help them navigate through these struggles. (An understanding of nontraditional students is important as well and will be addressed in Chapter 5.) Being well informed about changes in the attitudes, culture, trends, and values of students is important, as they may influence the developmental issues of students (Bishop, Lacour, Nutt, Yamada, & Lee, 2004). Today's students, for example, face unique psychosocial stressors resulting from the protracted recession in the country such as an ever-increasing burden of college debt and poor employment prospects (Berg-Cross & Green, 2010).

Because so many college counselors now believe that the traditional developmental struggles of college students have in many cases been superseded by more complex and serious psychological problems, college counselors need to possess strong skills in assessing and diagnosing more severe forms of psychopathology (Rudd, 2004; Sharkin & Coulter, 2005). It can be important to be well grounded in how to render a diagnosis using the latest edition of the *Diagnostic and Statistical Manual of Mental Disorders*, 4th ed. (*DSM-IV-TR*; American Psychiatric Association, 2000) given that nearly half of counseling centers recently surveyed reported that they generate a *DSM-IV* diagnosis (Barr et al., 2010). With increasing numbers of students requesting accommodations because of emotional and mental disabilities, college counselors may need to be prepared to review, evaluate, verify, and document such requests (Gibson, 2000). Even though many colleges now have offices devoted to disability services, college counselors may need to communicate or collaborate with these other service providers on campus. Other important skills include being able to discern psychopathology from developmentally based problems, knowing when to refer for evaluations for psychotropic medication, and knowing how and when to initiate hospitalization (Sharkin & Coulter, 2005). Also, as college counseling may increasingly adopt the model of evidence-based practice in which decisions about the care of clients are based on best available evidence, college counselors will need to keep abreast of research-based clinical evidence for treatment of specific disorders, such as anxiety and eating disorders (Cooper, 2005; Cooper et al., 2008).

In addition to clinical preparation, those who want to be college counselors need to develop skills in consulting and working collaboratively with several different constituencies (colleagues, personnel from other departments, administrators, professors, off-campus mental health professionals, and parents). In a sense, today's college counselor needs to be flexible, interpersonally skilled, and a team player as much as possible (Williams & Edwardson, 2000). There is a need to be well versed in the multiple missions of college counseling, including crisis intervention, consultation and outreach, and public health issues affecting college students (Bishop, 2006). Consultation and outreach is a particularly attractive skill desired by counseling center directors (Williams & Edwardson, 2000). Many college counselors are also expected to actively engage in scholarly writing and research projects, making research skills important.

For anyone who is considering a career in college counseling, it is reassuring to know that the work can be quite rewarding and satisfying professionally (Phelps, 1992; T. B. Smith et al., 2007), particularly because of the diversity in roles and activities that the work often entails (Hinkelman, 2005). Like most professions, college counseling is certainly not without its challenges and frustrations as well. In the next several chapters of this book, the reader will be provided with a true sense of the profession of college counseling and how vital it has become on today's campus.

Summary

There is a long, rich history of college counseling over the past several decades, as it has evolved into a unique profession with its own sense of professional identity and required skill set. The profession continues to expand and diversify, with growing numbers of practitioners coming from a variety of different training backgrounds. History shows that college counseling has been defined by an ability to adapt to the changing needs of the student population that it serves.

2

THE PRIMARY ROLES
AND RESPONSIBILITIES OF
COLLEGE COUNSELORS

The primary functions of college counselors can be divided into the following five categories: counseling, crisis intervention, consultation and outreach, training and supervision, and administrative duties. It is important to keep in mind that there can be significant variability from one counseling center to another in terms of how much time is devoted to these functions. The scope of services provided by a counseling center will depend on a number of factors, including the size of the institution, whether it is a public or private institution, whether it is largely a residential or commuter campus, and the number and expertise of counseling center staff. All college counselors must provide services in accordance with applicable ethical principles and standards set forth by the American Psychological Association (APA) (2002) and the American Counseling Association (ACA) (2005). Other ethical codes (e.g., for the National Association of Social Workers) would be relevant as well.

Counseling

Recent counseling center surveys (Barr, Rando, Krylowicz, & Winfield, 2010; Gallagher, 2010) indicate that about 10% of enrolled students will seek counseling on a given campus. The decision as to whether and what type of counseling is provided will depend on what services are available, criteria that suggest whether students are appropriate for counseling, and the type and severity of presenting problems of students. Generally speaking, positive criteria that suggest students are good candidates for counseling include presenting problems that are situational or developmental in nature, motivation to change, an ability to identify concerns and goals for counseling, a desire to achieve relief from symptoms, an ability to be introspective or insightful, and the capacity for developing a counseling relationship. Any previous counseling experiences characterized as positive or helpful by students is another indication that counseling is likely to be effective. Of course, many students will present with some but not all of these positive criteria, and some students may be deemed inappropriate for counseling services, for example, because of negative indicators such as poor motivation for counseling or need for more intensive services. Criteria for declining counseling and/or referring students to off-campus resources will be discussed in greater detail in Chapter 6.

College students seek counseling for a number of different problems. Some of the most common presenting concerns of college students are anxiety (including panic, post-traumatic stress, and social anxiety), depression, suicidal ideation and behavior, deliberate self-inflicted injury (such as cutting), substance abuse, and eating disorders (Sharkin, 2006). Other commonly observed problems include stress, relationship issues, family problems, academic difficulties, sexual concerns, and sexual victimization (including rape, sexual assault, sexual abuse in childhood, sexual harassment, stalking, and intimate partner violence) (Grayson & Meilman, 2006). Many of the problems with which students present are preexisting, for it has been noted that increasing numbers of students come to college with a history of mental health problems and previous treatment (Bishop, 2002; Sharkin, 2006). Again, the nature and severity of presenting problems that are beyond the expertise or resources of a college counseling center will require some students to be referred to community resources.

Individual and Group Counseling

All college counseling centers offer individual counseling, and this is clearly the professional activity college counselors engage in with the most frequency. On average, about 60% of a college counselor's time is devoted to direct service (Barr et al., 2010; T. B. Smith et al., 2007), and in most instances the majority of this time is used for one-on-one counseling for students (including intake interviews). On average, the typical full-time college counselor can expect to have a caseload of 26 client contact hours (Gallagher, 2010). On some campuses, individual counseling may also be provided to faculty and staff, though this may be on a very limited basis. Many campuses now offer employee assistance programs for staff and faculty, greatly reducing any need for them to seek assistance from campus counselors. Faculty and staff members may occasionally consult with counselors on campus to obtain information or referrals regarding personal or nonwork-related concerns.

As the primary modality, individual counseling is typically the most requested and expected service to be rendered by college counselors. Individual counseling is usually offered on a weekly or biweekly basis, with each session lasting approximately 50 minutes. The average number of sessions provided to students tends to be around six (Barr et al., 2010; Gallagher, 2010; Stone, Vespia, & Kanz, 2000). The demand for individual counseling will often exceed what can be realistically provided, particularly later in a semester, resulting in inevitable wait lists. Strategies for meeting the high demand and avoiding wait lists have been discussed and examined, such as using brief treatment or session limits (Ghetie, 2007; Tryon, 1995), referring students to outside services (Lacour & Carter, 2002), using a team-based clinical management system (Murphy & Martin, 2004), and using a clinical triage system (Rockland-Miller & Eells, 2006). Because the issue of meeting high demand for services with limited resources represents a serious challenge for college counseling, it will be addressed in more depth in Chapter 6.

Another way for college counselors with limited resources to meet the rising demand for services is to offer group counseling as an alternative to individual counseling (Golden, Corazzini, & Grady, 1993; Kincade & Kalodner, 2004; McEneaney & Gross, 2009; Parcover, Dunton, Gehlert, & Mitchell, 2006). Aside from it being an especially efficient use of resources, group counseling is generally perceived by college counselors as an effective mode of treatment for students. National surveys of counseling center directors have shown that an overwhelming majority of centers offer some type of group counseling (Golden et al., 1993; Williams & Edwardson, 2000). The format of the group can vary from structured psychoeducational topic groups to support groups to more general process-oriented psychotherapy groups.

Groups are often aimed at helping students with specific problems, such as eating disorders (Sheehy & Commerford, 2006), substance abuse (Meilman, Lewis, & Gerstein, 2006), social anxiety (Damer, Latimer, & Porter, 2010), grief (Berson, 1988; Knox, 2007), and earlier experiences of sexual abuse (Sack, Graham, & Simmons, 1995). Group counseling is considered by some to be the treatment of choice for students who present with relationship concerns (Whitaker, 2006). Groups can also be designed for specific subgroups of students such as gay, lesbian, and bisexual students (Chojnacki & Gelberg, 1995; Welch, 1996); international students (Walker & Conyne, 2007; Yau, 2004); nontraditionally aged students (25 and older) (Gary, 2007); students with disabilities (Corrigan, Jones, & McWhirter, 2001); student athletes (H. L. Harris, Altekruse, & Engels, 2003); students of color (Brown, Lipford-Sanders, & Shaw, 1995; Greer & White, 2008; Rollock, Westman, & Johnson, 1992; Wright, 1999); and multiracial students (Nishimura, 1998).

Traditionally, groups conducted by college counselors are cofacilitated, meet once weekly for 90 minutes, and consist of five to eight students on average (Golden et al., 1993). Students are typically prescreened to ensure that they are appropriate for group and may then also get some type of pregroup preparation (e.g., a handout with frequently asked questions about group) before they actually begin participating in a group. Although a vast majority of counseling centers offer group counseling, it may not necessarily be utilized by a significant percentage of clients (Golden et al., 1993). The challenges of filling groups has been attributed to student resistance to group involvement, groups being too narrowly focused in terms of recruiting members, and poor marketing efforts (Parcover et al., 2006). Staff attitude and motivation for doing group may also be a critical factor when trying to get groups started (Golden et al., 1993; Parcover et al., 2006). For example, centers in which group counseling is promoted as a primary treatment modality may have more success with running groups.

Couples and Family Counseling

Couples counseling is provided in many counseling centers, though much less frequently than individual and group counseling. Some centers may actively promote or highlight their couples counseling services, and some may have a training component for working with couples, which will naturally increase the volume of cases. Graduate students and nontraditionally aged undergraduates may be particularly apt to request couples or marital counseling. Couples counseling might be more appropriate than individual counseling under certain conditions (Whitaker, 2006). Centers may have policies regarding whether partners or spouses of students are eligible to be seen for couples sessions if they are not themselves enrolled as students.

The option of couples counseling could be explored with students whenever relationship troubles are a primary presenting concern and the partner is a fellow student. Some college counselors may avoid doing couples work even when it may be indicated simply because of their own anxiety about using a modality other than individual counseling. This fear may similarly arise when it comes to the idea of having family members participate in sessions with students. College counselors need not become experts in couples or family therapy but can acquire the proper training and experience to be able to provide these services on at least a limited basis.

The concept of doing family counseling in a college counseling center may seem counterintuitive given the quest of college students to generally establish increasing independence from their parents. However, encouraging family intervention or involving family members in a student's counseling has been advocated over the years (Baron, 1988; Beit-Hallahmi, 1974). This certainly seems to make sense based on the fact that family problems are often a presenting concern of students (Hargrove, McDaniel, Malone, & Christiansen, 2006), and family dysfunction has long been considered to have a strong influence on students' current problems (Witchel, 1991). Family-related concerns may play a particularly strong role in the lives of students of color (Jackson, 2009) and first-generation college students (Lippincott & German, 2007). Because family members are not always readily available or within a reasonable distance of the campus, some college counselors will use family therapy techniques with students (Baron, 1988; Hargrove et al., 2006; Terry, 1989), including the use of family systems strategies within group counseling (Vinson, 1995) and the use of genograms (Daughhetee, 2001; Vinson, 1995). Such techniques can elicit information about and promote insight into family dynamics and patterns within a student's family of origin (Daughhetee, 2001; Vinson, 1995).

Jackson (2009) provided a strong rationale for doing family therapy within the context of college counseling. She acknowledged that we now live in an era of "hovering" parents, sometimes referred to as "helicopter" parents, but rather than simply dismissing parents as too intrusive or overinvolved, college counselors can enlist parents as helpful allies in the treatment of student problems. Indeed, the behavior of so-called helicopter parents may actually contribute to many of the problems presented by students (Rettner, 2010), so why not involve them in the process in order to help improve communication and establish healthier boundaries? Jackson believes that it would benefit all college counselors to familiarize themselves with basic theories of family therapy and to consider family therapy as an appropriate modality when working with college students.

As the next subsection will address substance abuse counseling, it is interesting to mention here that amendments to FERPA over the past several years have allowed universities to notify parents of students under 21 years of age about student violations of policies on alcohol and drug use. This undoubtedly has opened the door for the potential for more involvement of parents in dealing with cases of student alcohol and drug abuse (Cutler, 2003).

Counseling for Substance Abuse and Other Addictions

Substance abuse among college students is well documented and is one of the more common reasons students end up in counseling (Meilman & Gaylor, 1989; Sharkin, 2006). Binge drinking and alcohol-related problems tend to be of primary concern on most college campuses. Unlike many of the other common problems of college students, substance abuse poses an especially unique challenge for college counselors because students referred to counseling for alcohol or other drug-related problems are often involuntary or mandated as a result of disciplinary or judicial sanctions. These sanctions are frequently due to secondary effects of alcohol or drug abuse, such as disorderly conduct, fighting, property damage, and other violations of student conduct. In contrast with voluntary clients, involuntary clients are much more likely to be reluctant, guarded, mistrustful, and in denial of any problem with little motivation to change (Sharkin, 2007). Needless to say, these are not ideal circumstances under which to provide counseling, and some counselors are, in fact, reluctant to see mandated clients (Sharkin, 2007; Stone & Lucas, 1994). This makes substance abuse or addictions counseling a unique type of counseling modality on many campuses.

The mandated nature of many of the substance abuse cases that come before college counselors will typically require some form of screening and assessment to identify problematic use of alcohol or other drugs (Gintner & Choate, 2007; Steenbarger, 1998). Depending on the outcome of these assessments, recommendations for counseling might be suggested, including individual counseling, group counseling, or participation in a psychoeducational group (Meilman et al., 2006). An intervention that has been used quite extensively with college students, especially for problem drinking, is motivational interviewing (Gintner & Choate, 2007; R. S. Harris, Aldea, & Kirkley, 2006; Meilman et al., 2006; Scholl & Schmitt, 2009; Steenbarger, 1998). This consists of interview strategies designed to minimize defensiveness and resistance, encourage students to find reasons to change, and reinforce efforts toward making change. Most cases of substance abuse counseling utilize brief interventions unless the level of alcohol or drug dependence is more severe, which would entail consideration of treatment off campus, including intensive outpatient or inpatient rehabilitation (Meilman et al., 2006).

In addition to alcohol and drug abuse, students may present with other forms of addiction, such as abuse of medications like Ritalin and Adderall, compulsive gambling (Petry, Weinstock, Morasco, & Ledgerwood, 2009), Internet addiction (Kandell, 1998), addiction to computer games, and different types of sexual addictions. Although students are more likely to seek treatment for these other addictions voluntarily (or at the urging of concerned others), college counselors can apply some of the same techniques used for substance abuse problems with similar effectiveness. College counselors will often-times encourage students to participate in self-help groups, such as Gamblers Anonymous and Sex Addicts Anonymous, as an additional support to counseling.

Another factor that makes addictions counseling on college campuses a distinct type of counseling is the use of specialists, particularly for alcohol and drug problems. Most college counselors will have at least enough background and experience to treat mild to moderate forms of substance abuse, but specialists may be better equipped for more troublesome cases. The typical specialist will be a certified addictions counselor in addition to having a more general background in counseling or a counseling-related field. Thus, these specialists do not have to be limited to seeing only substance abuse cases but can provide general counseling as needed. This is important because substance abuse typically involves co-occurring problems such as anxiety and depression (Meilman et al., 2006). Indeed, many students may use drugs or alcohol as a form of self-medication for emotional and psychological problems.

Academic Counseling

An important form of counseling provided by college counselors that is sometimes overlooked is academic counseling. Nearly half of the counseling centers in one survey indicated that they provide academic support services (Williams & Edwardson, 2000). While academic support services, such as study skills labs and writing centers, may be provided by others on campus, college counselors are in an advantageous position to intervene with students experiencing academic difficulties. College students often present in counseling with academic-related difficulties such as poor performance and failing grades, lack of motivation, poor study habits, mismanagement of time, and test anxiety. Moreover, in many cases mental-health-based problems cause disruption to students' academic functioning and performance (Sharkin, 2006). For example, academic performance can suffer as a result of depression (Brackney & Karabenick, 1995; Haines, Norris, & Kashy, 1996; Meilman, Manley, Gaylor, & Turco, 1992) and substance abuse (Kessler, Foster, Saunders, & Stang, 1995; Svanum &

Zody, 2001). Students may experience difficulties in their academic functioning because of situational stressors, such as illness, relationship troubles, family problems, legal troubles, and problems with roommates (Wlazelek & Hartman, 2007). Wlazelek and Hartman suggested that academic failure can represent a form of crisis for many students. It is certainly not surprising to think that forms of emotional or psychological stress or disturbance will have a negative impact on class attendance, concentration and memory, motivation, persistence, and general study habits. It has been estimated that close to 5% of college students fail to complete their education because of psychological problems (Kessler et al., 1995).

In addition to emotional disturbance, there can be myriad other reasons that students experience academic problems: lack of preparation or proper study skills for college-level work, deficiencies in specific domains (such as math or science), learning disabilities and attention deficit issues, mismatch between the student's preferred mode of learning and the particular educational system, lack of organizational skills, and lack of motivation for being in college or at a particular college (Ducey, 2006). In some instances, students find themselves in academic jeopardy because of competing demands such as athletics, employment, involvement in Greek organizations, and social activities (Wlazelek & Hartman, 2007).

There are a number of ways that college counselors can intervene to assist students with academic struggles. Before any intervention is made, however, college counselors need to conduct a thorough assessment of a student's academic functioning and performance, preferably at the point of entry into counseling (Wlazelek & Hartman, 2007). Depending on what is revealed by the assessment, assistance can be provided to help students with improving organizational and general study skills, managing time more effectively, managing test anxiety, managing stress associated with academic pressures, or improving test-taking strategies. Counselors can also help students improve sleep habits, given that poor sleep habits can result in missed classes and chronic tiredness. Intervention may need to focus on and explore underlying issues with motivation; for example, where there may be questionable motivation for why a student is currently in college or at a particular college. In addition to individual and group counseling modalities, college counselors can also help students with academic difficulties through workshops and outreach programs (Newton, 1990).

There is evidence to support the effectiveness of academic counseling provided by college counselors (Wlazelek & Coulter, 1999) and academic support seminars facilitated by college counselors (Newton, 1990) to help students in academic jeopardy. College counselors also help by encouraging students experiencing academic difficulties to take active steps to approach their professors and try to remedy their difficulties and, if appropriate, can serve as advocates to faculty on behalf of students. Of course, college counselors will refer students to academic support services provided by others on campus, such as tutoring and writing workshops, whenever appropriate.

Career Counseling

As was described in Chapter 1, career and vocational counseling was perhaps the main activity of college counselors in the early days of counseling centers. However, over the years career services increasingly became a separate service provided by others on campus (Cooper, Resnick, Rodolfa, & Douce, 2008). The changing nature of student problems and the need for college counselors to devote more time to serious forms of emotional and psychological distress has also contributed to less time being spent on career counseling. Despite these reported changes, one survey of counseling centers (Williams & Edwardson, 2000) found that nearly 60% of centers provided career counseling, and it was ranked by center directors as a "top ten" skill desired in new professionals. It has also been observed that today's students may be more oriented toward preparation for a career and financial success than ever before (Bishop, Lacour, Nutt, Yamada, & Lee, 2004). Thus, before drawing any false conclusions that career counseling is a dying component of college counseling, we must keep in mind that mental health problems and career development are intertwined and not mutually exclusive categories (Hinkelman & Luzzo, 2007; Zunker, 2008). Hinkelman and Luzzo suggested that psychological distress can exacerbate symptoms associated with career development, such as career indecision. In a similar manner, problems in the career development domain may contribute to significant emotional turmoil.

A case example may help demonstrate the close interrelationship between career development and emotional health. A student came to the counseling center in crisis because he was experiencing significant doubts about his current major and career path (in finance) just months before he was supposed to graduate. Much of the focus of the sessions revolved around how to resolve the dilemma of what may have been a mistake in his earlier choice of a major and eventual career path. Fortunately, he was able to resolve the crisis by arranging to switch to a different major (marketing and management) within the business college, which he felt comfortable with and extended his need to remain in school only by another semester or two.

This case illustrates how important it is for college counselors to remain vigilant to the interaction of vocational issues and psychological distress. Immediately referring a student to career services (if provided in a separate location) is not always the best course of action. It is important to note that this student agreed to allow communication between his counselor and his parents and subsequently agreed to have his parents come in for a family session because much of his distress was related to the fear of having to tell them about his dilemma. Conference calls with his parents during sessions and the session with his parents present served to alleviate much of his distress and enlisted their support in his decision to change his major and extend his time in school. Hence, this case also represents a good example of how involving family members in counseling can be advantageous.

A Note About Psychological Testing

Because counseling centers generally do not rely heavily on psychological testing in the provision of counseling services, it is not considered a primary activity of college counselors. When testing instruments are used, they tend to be simple single-construct measures (e.g., to assess for anxiety, depression, anger, disordered eating, etc.) or client problem checklists (Millon, Strack, Millon-Niedbala, & Grossman, 2008). However, psychological testing should at least be acknowledged as an activity that some college counselors use more so than others, depending on the background of the counselor and clinical philosophy of the counseling center. In addition, counseling centers that serve as training sites may incorporate testing into their training activities, including more extensive psychological batteries.

Examples of measures that are commonly used by college counselors include the Myers-Briggs Type Indicator and the Millon Clinical Multiaxial Inventory. These measures can be used to obtain and incorporate additional information about personality characteristics of clients into the counseling process. The utilization of assessment does require additional time for administration, scoring, and interpretation, which may be one reason why some college counselors use assessment sparingly. Despite the purported limited use of testing by college counselors, it is important to recognize that testing can be a valuable component of counseling. Indeed, Millon and his colleagues (2008) developed a multidimensional inventory, the Millon College Counseling Inventory, specifically for use with college students. This relatively new instrument can be used for intake assessment, treatment planning, and outcome assessment.

Crisis Intervention

Crisis intervention and emergency coverage is a critical component of counseling services provided on college campuses (Boyd et al., 2003), particularly for suicidal students (Silverman, 2006). Students deemed at risk for suicide represent the most common cases requiring college counselors to provide crisis intervention. Many aspects of college student suicide have been examined over the years, including demographic and other risk factors (Foreman, 1990; A. J. Schwartz & Whitaker, 1990; L. J. Schwartz & Friedman, 2009; Silverman, 2006; Silverman, Meyer, Sloane, Raffel, & Pratt, 1997; Westefeld et al., 2005), prevalence rates for students compared to nonstudents (Silverman, 2006; Silverman et al., 1997), the nature and prevalence of suicidal ideation (Drum, Brownson, Denmark, & Smith, 2009; Furr, Westefeld, McConnell, & Jenkins, 2001; Garlow et al., 2008; Westefeld et al., 2005), reasons students contemplate suicide (Drum et al., 2009; Westefeld et al., 2005; Westefeld, Whitchard, & Range, 1990), students' attitudes toward suicide (Westefeld et al., 1990,

2005), and assessment and treatment strategies (Foreman, 1990; A. J. Schwartz & Whitaker, 1990; L. J. Schwartz & Friedman, 2009; Silverman, 2006).

College student suicide became the focus of considerable media attention following the well-publicized suicide of MIT student Elizabeth Shin in 2000 and a string of suicides at NYU in 2003 and 2004 (Sharkin, 2006). These high-profile cases raised serious questions about if and when parents of suicidal students should be notified (Baker, 2005, 2006; Francis, 2003). Whether treatment for suicidal students should be mandated has been another controversial issue (Francis, 2003; Sharkin, 2007). Fear of liability over student suicide prompted some colleges to treat suicidal behavior as an infraction of student conduct codes requiring disciplinary sanctions (Appelbaum, 2006). This actually backfired, as some institutions were then sued for violating student rights. While schools are being more careful in how they handle suicidal students, concerns about student suicide have only heightened in recent times following the occurrence of six suicides at Cornell University during the spring term of 2010 (Levitt & Candiotti, 2010).

Of course, suicide is not the only reason that crisis intervention may be needed on a campus. There are a number of situations that might require an emergency or crisis intervention response: students who have panic attacks; students who are victims of assault, sexual assault, or rape; students who experience the death of a family member or someone else close to them; students who experience unwanted pregnancy; students who have psychotic episodes; students who have concerns about students who pose a danger to others; and students with crises involving substance abuse (e.g., blood alcohol poisoning). Students who engage in deliberate self-injury are often referred for crisis intervention by concerned others because they view the behavior as a form of suicidal behavior even though in reality students who self-injure are generally not suicidal (White, Trepal, Petuch, & Ilko-Hancock, 2007).

Crisis intervention can occur in several different ways: emergency walk-ins, urgent referrals, after-hours emergencies, and postvention in the aftermath of a death on or off campus. Each of these situations will be addressed separately. Once again, the reader needs to be cognizant that counseling centers vary in terms of what resources they have in place for crisis situations. For example, some campuses may have mental health emergency services on or close to campus (e.g., a hospital or crisis center) in addition to the counseling center.

Emergency Walk-ins

Perhaps the most common way that college counselors intervene in crisis situations occurs when students voluntarily come to the counseling center on an unscheduled or walk-in basis and request immediate assistance. Even though not all of these situations turn out to be actual emergencies, they are always treated as such in terms of making sure that these students are seen as soon as possible. It may be common to ask students if it is a true *emergency* or if they can wait at all before seeing a counselor, but the problem is that how one defines an emergency or crisis can differ tremendously from student to student. There may be times when students present as needing to speak to a counselor right away when in fact the urgency is for something on a relatively small scale compared with more serious situations. By the same token, students who are truly at risk can sometimes minimize their need for or appear as if they do not need immediate assistance.

Despite some "false alarms," it is likely that the majority of walk-ins are legitimate crisis situations, though not always involving suicidal risk. Clearly, the main objective is to ensure that there is no risk for suicide, self-harm, or harm to someone else. With suicidal students, there are specific protective measures that are commonly used, ranging from written safety plans or no-suicide contracts (Buelow & Range, 2001) to voluntary or involuntary hospitalization (Silverman, 2006). If the student is highly distressed but not suicidal, it is a matter of keeping the student calm and doing whatever possible to address and perhaps alleviate the distress.

Depending on the nature of the crisis, consultation with others on or off campus may be necessary. As an example, a student may miss an exam or not turn in an assignment on time because of being in distress (possibly related to academic difficulties), which might prompt the counselor to seek permission from the student to contact his or her professor. Intervention with a student who is disturbed by the behavior of a roommate would likely be referred to a dean or officials in residential life, or if deemed appropriate, the counselor would ask for permission to consult with these other individuals on the student's behalf. Regardless of the specific situation, at a minimum a follow-up session is usually arranged when seeing a nonsuicidal student in crisis, and oftentimes the crisis becomes the point of entry for participation in ongoing counseling.

One of the biggest challenges in dealing with walk-ins is having counselors available for immediate intervention. Some centers, especially at larger schools, will have emergency walk-in hours, but many centers do not have the staffing to be able to have walk-in hours set aside. Counseling centers must do the best they can with the resources they have in order to see all of the students who present in crisis.

Urgent Referrals

The second most common way that crisis intervention is initiated is when someone calls the counseling center with concerns about a student. These calls may come from students, professors, administrators, staff members in other offices on campus (e.g., health services, public safety, and residential life), and parents. In some scenarios, there will be a gap in time before the student is actually seen in the counseling center because efforts need to be made to contact and refer the student. In other scenarios, the concerned person is already with the student and will either escort or send the student over to the counseling center. Because of occasional instances of referred students never arriving at the counseling center, it is usually preferable for the concerned party to escort the student whenever possible.

As with walk-ins, these situations will be true emergencies in some cases and ones that do not necessarily qualify as such in other cases. Referral sources may not always have a good sense about what is and is not a true emergency, which is why college counselors are frequently called upon. A student crying is usually enough to arouse concern and compel someone to refer to the counseling center. Students who openly talk about past suicidal ideation or behavior, even when not currently at risk for suicide, will often arouse anxiety in others, who will then feel the need to make an immediate referral to counseling.

College counselors, therefore, must walk a delicate line between not wanting to overreact and at the same time not wanting to minimize the sense of urgency expressed by others.

One critical issue with referrals that come from others on campus (or from parents who call) is determining the need for obtaining student consent for release of information in order to follow up with the referral source. Because of restrictions on confidentiality of counseling, college counselors need to be careful not to inadvertently disclose information regarding a student without having the student's permission, ideally on a signed document. The practice of following up with people who refer students, especially under high concern or crisis conditions, can be helpful. Students can be encouraged to agree to such follow-ups and reassured that disclosures will be limited to what is deemed imperative for the referral source to know. Counselors can actually discuss and work with students on determining what should be shared. Students often show little resistance when asked for their consent to communicate with campus referral sources, particularly when it is primarily to confirm their contact with a counselor.

When parents are the ones who make the urgent referral, the situation can be trickier if students are reluctant to agree to allow the counselor to communicate with their parents. College counselors can easily get pulled into the dysfunctional family dynamics of students. In some cases, then, the most that students will agree to is simply confirming with the parent(s) that they were seen by the counselor. Anecdotally speaking, a vast majority of students specifically referred to counseling by parents seem to be okay with communication with their parents for follow-up purposes. This is especially true when parents are highly concerned and refer under what would be considered crisis conditions, for the students themselves usually understand why their parents felt the need to contact the counseling center.

After-Hours Emergencies

Many counseling centers provide after-hours on-call emergency services consisting of crisis management after regular office hours and on weekends (Coulter, Offutt, & Mascher, 2003; Gallagher, 2009; Meilman, Hacker, & Kraus-Zeilmann, 1993; Williams & Edwardson,

2000). College counselors may provide these services as an expected responsibility of their position without any additional compensation other than the possibility of compensatory time (Coulter et al., 2003; Gallagher, 2009). Counseling centers at larger institutions may have somewhat less actual involvement in after-hours emergencies because of the availability of other crisis services on and off campus (Coulter et al., 2003).

On the basis of a snapshot of one counseling center's on-call system, Meilman and his colleagues (1993) reported the occurrence of 50 on-call cases in one year (1991) for a student population of 7,600 students. They reported that most referrals were from health services and residential life staff, and follow-up counseling was initiated in 76% of cases. The time spent on a call can vary anywhere from several minutes to several hours. Meilman et al. found sexual assault cases to be the most time intensive, followed by cases of substance abuse and suicidal concerns.

After-hours crises may be referred by health services, campus police or public safety, or residential life. Although the majority of cases may involve concerns about potential suicide risk, other common on-call situations might involve panic attacks, substance abuse, self-injurious behavior, sexual assault, or concerns about potential violence or aggression against others. Some may simply be cases of students in distress who either ask to speak to a counselor or are referred to the on-call counselor (similar to urgent referrals made during regular office hours). When emergency calls concern students who reside on campus, counselors may be asked to make an assessment not only of the student's current emotional state and level of risk but also of whether it will be safe for the student to remain in his or her residence hall, at least for that night or through the weekend.

While the provision for after-hours emergency coverage is an essential component of many college counseling centers and enhances the "perceived" value of counseling services on a campus (in the eyes of administrators), it is probably the least popular and most taxing aspect of the work (Coulter et al., 2003). Responding to student crises during regular working hours can be stressful enough, but trying to deal with a crisis situation in the middle of the night can be even more daunting. Even when no crisis calls are received, the experience of just being on-call requires one to always be psychically prepared for something, which in and of itself can be somewhat emotionally taxing.

Postvention

The need for intervention can emerge in the aftermath of a student death, suicide, or near-death, which is commonly referred to as *post-vention* (Meilman & Hall, 2006; Petretic-Jackson, Pitman, & Jackson, 1996; Philip, 1990; Swenson & Ginsberg, 1996). On some campuses, the postvention will be initiated by a campus-based crisis response team (Streufert, 2004). There may be situations, however, in which college counselors will be proactive or reactive in such postvention efforts without the utilization of a designated team response per se (Philip, 1990). There are many factors that will influence the need for and nature of college counselor involvement following the death or suicide of a student. Of particular importance is determining which individual students (e.g., friends, roommates, etc.) and student groups (e.g., Greek organization, club, athletic team, residence hall, etc.) are most affected by the student's death. College counselors may be asked to intervene in several capacities, such as meeting with groups of affected students, consulting with staff and faculty, being present at vigils or memorial services that take place on campus, and being available for emergency counseling sessions.

Interventions in the aftermath of a suicide or suicide attempt can be quite challenging because of complicated emotional and grief reactions. This is particularly true if the attempted or completed suicide occurs on campus and/or is actually witnessed by other students. This can result in a range of emotional reactions, including shock and disbelief, sadness and guilt, and anger and resentment (e.g., due to the upheaval this caused in their lives). All of these emotional reactions are common and reflect the various ways that individuals react and cope with traumatic experiences.

Deaths of staff and faculty members can similarly result in significant distress among students, colleagues, and others, especially when sudden and unexpected. J. M. Davis, Bates, and Velasquez (1990) described a postvention model based on the suicide of a fellow faculty member in their department of counselor education that affected faculty, administrators, and students alike. This was particularly devastating because it involved a member of the department of counselor education, for people tend to erroneously assume that those who work in the counseling profession are somehow more immune to depression and suicide.

In contrast with counseling, which typically takes place behind "closed doors," crisis intervention can be a more visible dimension of the work that college counselors perform. When college counselors are contacted by others to intervene with distressed and potentially at-risk students, they will often need to conduct their interventions with the assistance (and perhaps presence) of these concerned parties or referral sources. This is an opportunity for college counselors to demonstrate, at least on one level, the value of their knowledge and skills in the campus setting. This visibility factor is especially salient when college counselors need to conduct a postvention or respond to a larger scale crisis on campus.

Consultation and Outreach

Consultation and outreach represent critical activities of college counselors on today's campus. *Consultation* is typically provided to students, faculty, staff, administrators, and parents and tends to revolve around concerns about the well-being of specific students.

Outreach entails activity that literally takes counselors outside of their offices and into the campus community, presenting psychoeducational and prevention programs. Outreach is most often provided to students but can be provided to others within the campus community. Both of these activities are required for accreditation by the International Association of Counseling Services (IACS) (Boyd et al., 2003) and ranked as highly desired skills that center directors look for in new hires (Williams & Edwardson, 2000).

Consulting With Others on Campus

Phone calls from students, professors, staff members (especially in health services and residential life), and administrators are a common occurrence in the life of college counselors. Students will sometimes contact the counseling center to consult with a counselor about their own situation, which may then result in the scheduling of an appointment to meet, but often will call to consult regarding another student (i.e., a friend, boyfriend or girlfriend, or roommate). When the call involves a student concerned about another student, college counselors will provide support and make suggestions for helping and referring the student to counseling. In situations where there is concern about potential high risk, steps will be taken to ensure that the student is contacted directly and evaluated as soon as possible. It is only in rare instances that a student will not want to give the other student's name, for most students recognize that nothing can be done without fully cooperating.

The most common calls that come from faculty and staff members in other offices are to express concern about a specific student and request suggestions for assisting and referring the student to counseling. It follows essentially a similar protocol as when a student calls about another student. The counselor will suggest ways to encourage the student to make an appointment, or the caller will be encouraged to escort the student to the counseling office. The process tends to work best when the concerned party calls with the student present in his or her office, and there is a willingness on the student's part to come over to the counseling center voluntarily. With students who are more reluctant, the counselor may need to simply speak with them over the phone to make an assessment of their current emotional state and level of risk. College counselors will sometimes agree to meet with a student where the student is currently rather than have the student come to the counseling center if the student is too upset or unwilling to come. In some instances, the concerned party will make this request. For example, a professor may request that the counselor see a student in his or her office rather than have to escort the student to the counseling center.

College counselors sometimes receive calls regarding students who are current or former clients of the counseling center. Without having a student's consent, counselors cannot confirm or deny this during these calls because of restrictions of confidentiality, although in some instances students will themselves reveal this information to the concerned party. In general, college counselors always need to be mindful of confidentiality when consulting with others on campus about students. Nowadays most faculty and staff seem to have an understanding about the confidentiality of counseling, but that does not mean that they will not still try to seek information at times.

In some instances, a call from a concerned party can be somewhat complicated and may require the counselor to involve other campus personnel. As an example, there was a case in which a professor called the counseling center to report that one of her students came to see her after class because he had done poorly on an exam that had just been returned. After she informed the student that there was nothing that could be done to improve his grade on the exam (or his overall performance in the class to that point), he made a comment that he might as well kill himself and then left her office. After the student left, the professor called the counseling center. She did not characterize it as an urgent matter, sensing that the student had simply made a flippant remark, but she decided she should contact the counseling center so that someone could follow up with the student and make sure he was not suicidal.

The counselor who consulted with the professor explained that the counseling center was not in the best position to intervene given that the student had left her office and his whereabouts were currently unknown. Instead, it was recommended that public safety be contacted so that they could try to locate the student, conduct a welfare check, and if necessary escort him to the counseling center to be evaluated. Even though the counselor offered to make the call to public safety, the professor became upset because she considered involvement of public safety to be too strong a response given the situation. The professor thought that the counselor could contact the student directly. The counselor reiterated that the only way to ensure that the student could be properly evaluated for suicide risk was to involve public safety, but the professor was clearly not happy with the counselor's response. The professor relented, and public safety was contacted. Public safety officers soon found the student as he exited a class. When he was asked about his comment in the professor's office, he reported that it was meant as a joke, and he had no intention of committing suicide. It was later discovered that the student had been diagnosed with Asperger's syndrome (a disorder on the autism spectrum, which will be discussed in Chapter 3) and was prone to make inappropriate comments as he did with his professor.

This example shows that not all consultations are simple and that the concerned person who calls to consult with a counselor may be dissatisfied with the process or outcome of the call. Furthermore, it is an example of an all too common phenomenon related to consultations with others on campus and parents: There may be an unrealistic expectation of what the counselor or counseling center can do in a particular situation. College counselors should generally avoid putting themselves in the position of contacting or coercing students to meet with them, especially before they are clients of the counseling center. This can be a violation of ethics and is clearly a role that may be best assumed by others on campus, such as the dean of students. Nevertheless, there will continue to be consultative calls in which counselors are expected to intervene directly with students who arouse concern. Thus, these consultations often require college counselors to inform concerned parties about what is and is not an appropriate way to intervene depending on the specific circumstances.

Consulting With Parents

It is common for college counselors to receive calls from parents who are concerned about the mental health of their sons and daughters. Calls might originate from parents of students who have not yet been to the counseling center or from parents of students who are already clients. When parents of nonclients call, it is usually straightforward. They call expressing specific concerns about the emotional or psychological well-being of their children and seek advice on what to do. Many of these calls eventually result in students being referred to counseling. With student consent, follow-up contact with parents who refer students to counseling is often helpful and certainly appreciated by parents.

When the parents of current clients call, the situation can be a bit more challenging for counselors. It is most troublesome in cases in which students have poor or conflicted relationships with their parents and prefer they not have any involvement in the counseling process. Some parents will be quite demanding and insist on having their say and influence in the counselor's interaction with the student. There can be positive and negative aspects of dealing with parents of troubled students (Sharkin, 2006), but the bottom line is that except in circumstances where the parents are clearly part of the student's troubles (e.g., abusive parents), college counselors need to work with parents as much as possible. As described earlier, family interventions not only are appropriate in many cases but can also go a long way toward helping resolve distress in students' lives. The trick for college counselors is to find the right balance between enlisting the support and input of parents and being mindful of and sensitive to the student's privacy and boundary issues within the family.

College counselors often find themselves walking a fine line in this regard. It is not hard to imagine how challenging it can be to be responsive to concerned parents of a client while respecting the student's wish not to involve parents in the counseling. The counselor should never ignore calls from parents even when the student refuses to give the counselor consent to share information with the parents. As noted earlier, counselors can easily get pulled into dysfunctional family dynamics, and thus it is imperative for counselors to manage these boundaries as best as possible. For example, counselors may need to come to some type of mutually agreed-upon arrangement in cases in which students do not wish to involve their parents but the parents repeatedly call with their concerns.

Outreach for Students

In contrast with the practice of consultation, which primarily occurs in the counseling center (oftentimes by telephone), outreach almost always involves going outside the counseling center. Outreach is an activity that is most commonly conducted for students. There are several different goals and purposes of conducting outreach for students on campus. First, outreach can be used to share information about counseling services and how to access the counseling center. This may include programs to orient students (particularly first-year students) to the counseling process in order to destigmatize counseling and lessen anxiety about the prospect of seeking counseling (Hayes et al., 2008). A majority of counseling centers report that they participate in new student orientation programs (Gallagher, 2010), which can be an especially critical time to inform incoming students about counseling services. Outreach designed to provide information about counseling can be useful in reaching out to students who may be in distress yet do not seek counseling because they are unaware of counseling services and how to use them (Yorgason, Linville, & Zitzman, 2008). Hayes et al. (2008) actually used a mock session to show how a counseling appointment is made and what the initial session is like.

Second, psychoeducational programs can be presented in classes, residence halls, fraternities and sororities, and other campus settings for the purpose of prevention and to educate students about relevant topics. Topics can fall within one of three domains: educational-career, personal-social, and health-related (Kern, 2000). Examples of educational-career topics include test anxiety, study skills, goal setting, time management, learning styles, the first-year experience, the senior transition experience, and how to choose a career. Popular personal-social topics are stress management, dating and relationships, sexuality, body image, coping with anxiety, coping with depression, suicide prevention, anger management, improving communication skills, assertiveness, overcoming shyness, learning how to resolve conflict, preventing date and acquaintance rape, and boosting self-esteem. Common health-related subjects are substance abuse, healthy eating, exercise, sleeping well, sexually transmitted diseases, and practicing safe sex. Even when well planned and organized, it can be challenging to ensure good attendance at a presentation that is done outside of a classroom setting. Strong attendance at outreach presentations can never be completely guaranteed when it comes to college students, but presentations that are well publicized and incorporated in course curricula (as an incentive to earn extra credit) can help increase attendance (Marks & McLaughlin, 2005; Schreier & Bialk, 1997). Obtaining cosponsorship from a student group or organization can also help produce good attendance.

Third, outreach represents a way to serve students who may be hesitant to seek counseling. Outreach programs can help make counseling seem more accessible and inviting to students who are less inclined to initiate counseling but could potentially benefit from it. One way that counseling centers have attempted to make their services more accessible is to set up a counselor-in-residence program in which direct services are offered in the residence halls by professional staff (H. Davis, Kocet, & Zozone, 2001; Halstead & Derbort, 1988; S. Harris, 1994). Rawls, Johnson, and Bartels (2004) expanded on the traditional counselor-in-residence model by making consultation and support for residential life staff the primary function while still providing counseling and crisis intervention. Some college counselors have found success with programs designed to serve students unlikely to use counseling by employing a combination of advising (to staff and faculty who have regular contact with the students), advocacy in situations involving environmental stressors, and provision of "support" as opposed to more traditional counseling (Mier, Boone, & Shropshire, 2009).

Sometimes it is appropriate to offer a specific type of program to a specific group of students. As an example, sexual assault programs have been designed specifically for men in fraternities (Choate, 2003). Another example would be a program for adult students and/or graduate students on the challenges of balancing multiple roles. Outreach can also be in the form of campus-wide events and programs aimed at assessing and helping students with specific problems. For example, college counselors will lend their expertise to national screening days and awareness-week campaigns that offer information, presentations, and quick assessments on different types of psychological disorders. These events help raise awareness of the risk factors and symptoms of specific disorders and how to get professional help. Some examples include National Eating Disorders Awareness Week (in February), National Anxiety Disorders Screening Day (in May), National Suicide Prevention Week (in September), National Depression Screening Day (in October), National Collegiate Alcohol Awareness Week (in October), and Mental Health Wellness Week (in November). College counselors also frequently participate in health and wellness fairs on campus that promote ways for students to maintain healthy lifestyles and manage their stress.

In addition to the aforementioned events, college counselors routinely participate in programs devoted to sexual assault awareness and prevention on their campuses. In Pennsylvania, the Department of Education passed legislation requiring new guidelines for sexual violence education on campuses. These new guidelines are intended to ensure that all campuses within the state have violence education programs in place. Around the country, many campuses have long been involved in activities aimed at sexual violence education, such as the Clothesline Project and Take-Back-the-Night rally (R. W. Lee, Caruso, Goins, & Southerland, 2003). The Clothesline Project allows students to paint brief messages about sexual assault on T-shirts, which are then displayed on campus. Take-Back-the-Night is an event in which students rally and then march (sometimes in a candlelight vigil) to protest against sexual violence. There are also programs aimed at changing attitudes of and enlisting the support of men in efforts to prevent sexual (and domestic) violence (Fabiano, Perkins, Berkowitz, Linkenbach, & Stark, 2003), such as "Men Against Violence," "Men Can Stop Violence," and "Walk a Mile in Her Shoes." College counselors can commonly become involved in these projects as part of their outreach efforts. They also design and run programs on relationship violence, with topics ranging from risky behaviors to dating violence.

A final purpose of outreach is that it is an ideal way for college counselors to be more visible on campus. Given that college counselors spend a significant amount of their daily time in private individual and group counseling sessions, it is important for them to be visible on the campus as much as possible. There can sometimes be a sense of mystery and secretiveness that students associate with counseling, so it can help for counselors to be more visible on campus as a way to demystify the counseling center and make it seem less threatening. Increased visibility can also come in the form of campus or local news articles. College counselors are frequently asked to give interviews for news articles on college student mental-health-related issues or specific events such as the Virginia Tech shootings or a suicide on their campus. This represents another important way for college counselors to give information about who they are and the type of services they provide. Also, if they participate in certain types of programming, it can show students that they are interested in and competent in those areas. For example, helping with multicultural events may make culturally diverse students more comfortable to seek help from that counselor or in general.

On some campuses, college counselors have employed peer education programs in which students are trained to facilitate or cofacilitate outreach programs to their peers (Ender & Newton, 2000). Having students serve as ambassadors of the counseling center is another means of making the counseling center more accessible and student friendly. Peer educators can be used to address a number of topics such as eating disorders (Sesan, 1988–89), health education (Sloane & Zimmer, 1993), communication skills for roommates (Waldo, 1989), dating violence (J. P. Schwartz, Griffin, Russell, & Frontaura-Duck, 2006), and diversity awareness (J. M. Nolan, Levy, & Constantine, 1996). Peer educators can be utilized for health fests, awareness weeks, and similar programs where they can interact with and invite student peers to participate. Student peer educators can infuse outreach programming with a unique energy and enthusiasm, though overseeing a peer education program does require considerable time and resources to recruit, select, train, and supervise student volunteers (Lindsey, 1997). It can be especially challenging to work with a group of students who serve on a voluntary basis (e.g., maintaining regular attendance at meetings); therefore, it can make a significant difference if there are funds available to hire students as opposed to enlisting only volunteers.

Outreach for Faculty and Staff

Outreach is not aimed solely at students. College counselors conduct presentations and workshops for faculty and staff in order to help them in the identification of and intervention with emotionally distressed students (Ellingson, Kochenour, & Weitzman, 1999; J. M. Nolan, Ford, Kress, Anderson, & Novak, 2005; Rodolfa, 1987; Sharkin, 2006). These presentations will generally focus on common forms of student distress, warning signs of distress, and how to make a referral for counseling. Programs specifically for faculty can also be used to address how to handle problems with academic dishonesty (Brilliant & Gribben, 1993) and disruptive students in the classroom (De Lucia & Iasenza, 1995; Hernandez & Fister, 2001). New faculty and staff orientation and departmental meetings represent ideal opportunities for doing brief yet informative presentations.

As with students, faculty and staff members are susceptible to misinformation, misperceptions, or lack of understanding of counseling services (Bishop, Bishop, & Beale, 1992; Much, Wagener, & Hellenbrand, 2010) though they do tend to understand how mental health issues can negatively influence academic functioning (Backels & Wheeler, 2001). Thus, doing outreach programs for faculty and staff is an important way for college counselors to not only share their knowledge and expertise with them but also ensure that the people most likely to encounter troubled students are well informed of the services available and how to help students access them.

Outreach does not necessarily need to be in the form of doing presentations, which can be challenging to arrange, given the demanding schedules of faculty and staff members. Outreach can be in the form of brochures and other publications. S. A. Nolan, Pace, Iannelli, Palma, and Pakalns (2006) developed a guide that is mailed to faculty members along with counseling center brochures. The guide includes information about student problems that might warrant a referral to counseling and helpful tips about how to refer students. Nolan et al. reported that the distribution of the guide actually led to an increase in the number of referrals from faculty. Many counseling centers have designed and distributed similar guides or handbooks for faculty as well as staff, and many post these materials on their websites.

Coordinating of Outreach Programming

Although it is not necessary, depending on the size and functions of a particular counseling center, it can be helpful to have someone within a center be designated as the outreach coordinator (OC). The more active a center is in outreach activity, the more necessary it might be to have someone in this role. An OC can be responsible for fielding requests for presentations and programs, ensuring that each requested program is assigned, and promoting outreach programming as a key component of service delivery. Moreover, an OC can explore opportunities for collaborative efforts with other offices and student groups on campus and ways to market or advertise outreach to the campus community. Other important activities that the OC might be responsible for include the compilation of materials to be used for outreach (e.g., handouts and pamphlets), maintenance of a calendar for outreach programs during the academic year, and collection of data from programs conducted (e.g., attendance, evaluations, etc.). In terms of outreach materials, the OC can post requests for materials or resources that other college counselors have developed and used, so as to not have to "reinvent the wheel" for each new outreach endeavor. These postings can be on LISTSERVs, forums, and discussion groups, such as those of the American College Counseling Association, all of which represent ideal ways for college counselors to share resources. There is also the Counseling Center Village (counselingcentervillage.com), which was created specifically for counseling center professionals and contains a treasure trove of workshop designs, handouts, evaluation forms, and other valuable material. In general, having someone serve as an OC can assist in a center's overall effort to be responsive to requests for outreach and to be proactive in offering campus-wide programs.

Training and Supervision

Surveys of counseling centers (Barr et al., 2010; Williams & Edwardson, 2000) have found that 75% of them serve as training sites or have some form of training program. The training and supervision of practicum students, predoctoral interns, and postdoctoral residents and fellows is considered by the IACS to be an important and desirable component of counseling centers (Boyd et al., 2003). College counseling centers are well represented among predoctoral internship settings, with nearly 100 counseling centers currently approved as internship sites by the American Psychological Association. Although supervision provided in counseling centers is typically for trainees, it should be pointed out that new hires in counseling centers are often expected to receive supervision (usually from the director or other senior staff member) and may prefer to have regular supervision (Coll, 1995). New professionals may also need supervised clinical hours to be eligible for licensure.

Given the significant role that counseling centers often play in the training and supervision of counselor trainees, many college counselors are likely to serve as supervisors at some point in, if not throughout, their career. Some college counselors, particularly in centers that are accredited as predoctoral internship sites, will assume primary duties associated with training and have the title of training director.

Although the specific duties will vary depending on the size and scope of training in a particular center, the general role of the training director is to coordinate the center's training program and activities, which will usually include facilitating a seminar or group meeting of all of the trainees at the same time. The training director will typically oversee the recruitment of prospective trainees, the application and selection process for choosing new trainees, and the evaluation of the training program. The training director will typically serve as the point of contact for academic training coordinators at universities from which trainees are selected.

At a minimum, training programs in counseling centers will consist of individual supervision provided to trainees, and those centers that have multiple trainees may also include some type of group supervision, training seminar, or case presentation forum for the trainees. Accredited training programs for predoctoral interns and postdoctoral residents need to fulfill a specific set of training experiences in order to meet accreditation standards (American Psychological Association, Committee on Accreditation, 2007; Association of Psychology Postdoctoral and Internship Centers, 2006).

All training programs must meet minimum standards. Clients assigned to trainees must be appropriate for their level of training (Boyd et al., 2003); trainees need to be supervised closely by experienced, qualified staff (Boyd et al., 2003); there should be sufficient time to adequately oversee all cases assigned to trainees (Falvey, 2002); and there should be a protocol in place in the event that trainees experience clients in crisis (Hipple & Beamish, 2007). In addition, there should always be a training agreement or supervision contract that clearly spells out the goals, expectations, objectives, responsibilities, and requirements of the supervised training experience (Osborn & Davis, 1996; Sharkin & Coulter, 2009). An example of what should be included in such a contract can be found in Sharkin and Coulter (2009). A related issue is the importance of early and ongoing communication between college counselor supervisors and academic faculty from trainees' programs to ensure that trainees have positive and productive training experiences (Sharkin & Coulter, 2009). In addition to the ethical codes of professional associations such as ACA and APA, ethical guidelines for the practice of supervision are delineated by the Association for Counselor Education and Supervision (1993), which is a division of ACA.

There are various models of supervision, some of which have been applied to college counseling, such as the Supervisory Working Alliance Model (Wood, 2005) and the use of computer-based feedback during sessions (also known as the bug-in-the-eye method) (K. L. Miller, Miller, & Evans, 2002). Such models of supervision can be helpful in terms of providing a framework for how to supervise the clinical work of trainees. Also, it has been recommended that counseling centers incorporate principles of evidence based practice into their training programs (Owen, Tao, & Rodolfa, 2005) given the increasing need in clinical settings to utilize treatment techniques that have been shown to be effective. Supervisors of trainees in a counseling center may also need to be cognizant of multiple interacting subsystems that exist within the larger counseling center system (Brunk, 1991).

An additional consideration for counseling centers that serve as training sites is the importance of balancing training needs against service needs (Scanlon & Gold, 1996; Sharkin & Coulter, 2009). There can be a tendency to rely on trainees to help meet high demand, but centers must remain mindful of the primary purpose of trainees being in the center, which is to learn and develop clinical skills. IACS cautions that centers must be careful not to allow training to supersede their primary mission as a provider of services to students (Boyd et al., 2003). There is no doubt that having trainees can allow a center to see more clients, perhaps better meeting the demand for services and avoiding the need to use a wait list, but trainees should never be exploited specifically for this purpose.

Another type of training and supervision that can occur in a college counseling center is the use of paraprofessionals, namely, students who serve as peer counselors. In contrast with peer educators who conduct outreach programs, peer counselors usually assume a pseudocounseling role with their peers. Examples of this would be the use of peer counselors to serve as therapeutic aides to eating disorder clients (Lenihan & Kirk, 1990) and peer counselors trained to teach basic social skills to peers trying to overcome shyness (Booth, 1990). It is also common to use peer counselors to serve on campus-based hotlines, to help with orientation programs, and to assist peers with study skills. Although some counseling centers continue to run peer counseling programs, they can require a lot of training and pose unique risks given the more intimate nature of contact the peer counselors have with fellow students. Based on a review of the literature, it appears that the heyday of peer counseling may be well in the past, perhaps a reflection of the changing nature of student problems over the years and growing concerns about liability risk. Just to show how much times have changed, an older journal article by Bernard, Roach, and Resnick (1981) described a training workshop for students who worked as campus bartenders to serve in a paraprofessional capacity while tending bar. It is hard to imagine anything like that in today's world.

Administrative Duties

A vital yet often unrecognized aspect of the everyday professional life of college counselors is the need to attend to administrative tasks. Of course, the director of a counseling center will have the primary administrative responsibilities, for she or he is expected to oversee the overall administration of the office. The administrative duties of the director are delineated by IACS (Boyd et al., 2003) and include strategic planning and goal setting, resource allocation, management of the budget, supervision of support staff, setting the agenda for staff meetings, evaluation of services, completion of annual reports, and compilation of accountability data for senior-level administrators. Most if not all directors will rely to some degree on their professional staff to assist with these and other administrative duties. In fact, it is recommended that all professional staff be involved in the development and implementation of policies and procedures (Eells, Seals, Rockett, & Hayes, 2005). Many directors will seek assistance from their staff and colleagues on issues ranging from budgetary matters to the editing of annual reports. Needless to say, being a director of a counseling service can be stressful (Ross, 1995), especially dealing with the challenge of fostering and maintaining staff morale as well as budgetary concerns (Eells et al., 2005; Herr, Heitzmann, & Rayman, 2006). As the old adage goes, it can be "lonely at the top."

In many counseling centers (especially larger ones) staff members may be designated to serve as associate or assistant director, training director, clinical services coordinator, crisis services coordinator, group counseling coordinator, assessment and testing coordinator, and outreach coordinator. Someone may be assigned primary responsibility for computer-programming issues, such as maintenance of software scheduling programs and the compilation of database statistics. Some centers may assign a staff member to serve as multicultural services coordinator (or liaison) in order to coordinate efforts to reach out to and foster relationships with underserved student groups on campus.

Because of the high volume of cases that many counseling centers are experiencing, some may opt to hire full-time case managers rather than rely on a staff member with limited time to serve as coordinator of clinical services. Essentially, case managers can devote themselves full-time to important administrative functions related to clinical services. The primary role of a case manager could be to oversee the scheduling and management of counseling services. This may include activities such as assigning clients for counseling after their initial evaluation, contacting clients regarding missed appointments, maintaining wait lists for counseling, and assisting clients with accessing off-campus services.

One of the most important administrative tasks of college counselors is to document all contacts with clients and others who consult about clients and nonclients. These contacts can be done face-to-face, by telephone, and by electronic mail. It is crucial for counselors to maintain records that are ethically, legally, and clinically sound (Luepker, 2003; R. W. Mitchell, 2007). When supervising trainees, college counselors need to carefully review and sign off on their supervisees' records, and records should be kept of the supervision sessions as well. Record keeping is essential for many reasons but particularly for ensuring quality and continuity of care. The increasing reliance on electronic record keeping in counseling centers can pose unique challenges to confidentiality; therefore, this form of record keeping will be further addressed in Chapter 6.

Summary

The primary roles of college counselors are in the domains of counseling (in a number of different modalities including individual, group, couples, family, academic, and career), crisis intervention, consultation, outreach programming, training and supervision, and administrative responsibilities such as record keeping. Most college counselors will devote the majority of their time to these activities, though there can be varying amounts of time spent within each domain depending on the needs and resources of the counseling center. In addition to these primary duties, college counselors contribute their time to other important functions on their campuses; these additional roles will be explored in Chapter 3.

3

ADDITIONAL ROLES AND CONTRIBUTIONS ON CAMPUS

College counselors participate in activities beyond their primary duties that can have an important impact on their campuses. This chapter will explore some of these additional roles in which college counselors support the educational mission of their universities. Specifically, this chapter will examine how college counselors (a) serve as academic advisers to students; (b) provide assistance to students with learning disabilities and attention deficit disorder; (c) provide assistance to students with autism spectrum disorders; (d) contribute to the overall retention effort of their universities; (e) serve on intervention teams for identifying at-risk and disruptive students, identifying and reducing potential campus threats, and providing coordinated response to crises; (f) serve on university committees and task forces; and (g) teach undergraduate- and graduate-level courses.

Academic Advising

Academic advising is a vitally important service provided to students on any campus (Alexitch, 2006). Faculty members tend to serve as the primary (and sometimes only) academic advisors on campuses, but more and more colleges and universities have been turning to others to assist in the process of advising students. Many campuses now have advising centers with professional staff whose primary duty is to advise students with academic issues such as selecting courses and fulfilling curriculum requirements (Self, 2008). Professional academic advising is itself a profession with a national association (National Academic Advising Association) that has been growing fast (Self, 2008). There are certainly advantages to having professional staff members available who can be fully devoted to advising, but this is not always feasible for institutions, particularly during tough economic times.

While academic advising is not always as formal with college counselors as it may be with professional advisors, college counselors will inevitably find themselves doing some advising with students. College counselors may often find themselves helping students figure out what courses might be in their best interest to enroll in, what major they might want to declare, whether to switch to another major, and if and when to drop courses. Of course, it is important for counselors to refer students to others, namely, faculty or professional advisors (if available), so as not to overstep the boundaries of what they are qualified to do on campus. For college counselors who have faculty rank and privileges, this is less of a problem than it might be for counselors who do not have faculty status.

Self (2008) observed that counselors are known to serve as advisors, particularly at community colleges and smaller campuses, because they are well suited for the task of advising. Self pointed out that many counselors are well informed about academic curriculum and programs so that they can serve competently as advisors. Some students may actually prefer to seek academic advising from college counselors rather than faculty members if they perceive their counselor to be especially trustworthy and supportive as well as knowledgeable about academic issues.

Assisting Students With Learning Disabilities and ADHD

With increasing numbers of students with learning disabilities (LDs) and attention-deficit/hyperactivity disorder (ADHD) coming to college, most institutions of higher education have disability support services and programs in place to ensure compliance with the Americans With Disabilities Act. Even though many campuses now have specialists to work with students with varying types of disabilities, this does not mean that counseling centers no longer have a role in providing assistance to these students. In one survey, 18% of counseling centers reported that they provided disability support services (Williams & Edwardson, 2000), and generally speaking, students with disabilities will often seek or be referred for counseling.

Undoubtedly, many college counselors have the knowledge and skills to effectively assist and work with students who have LDs and/or ADHD. This is especially true, given that many problems associated with LDs (e.g., impulsivity, disorganization, and self-esteem struggles) and problems associated with ADHD (e.g., mood disorders and substance abuse) are problems commonly addressed in counseling. In many cases, college counselors may provide assistance in conjunction with other campus or off-campus professionals such as LD specialists.

There are several ways that college counselors can help students with LDs. College counselors can help students deal with feelings of inferiority and shame that are related to LD diagnoses, help students develop a sense of self-worth, teach students coping strategies and how to advocate for themselves, and aid students in the acquisition of proper accommodations (Bergin & Bergin, 2007). Some of the basic techniques of academic counseling discussed earlier are commonly used with students with LDs. There may be cases in which it is important for college counselors to serve as advocates for students with LDs, for example, by consulting and educating faculty about the academic struggles for college students with LDs. This is sometimes necessary to counteract the negative attitudes held by some faculty about having to make accommodations for students with LDs (Beilke & Yssel, 1999; Vogel, Leyser, Wyland, & Brulle, 1999). Support groups can be particularly effective in providing emotional support (Dinklage, 1991) and for promoting acceptance of having an LD as well as coping with the social stigma that is often associated with having an LD (Wilczenski, 1992).

Unlike LDs, ADHD symptoms may first emerge when or not be diagnosed until students are in college. With ADHD, it is important for college counselors to do a thorough assessment and evaluation (Ramsay & Rostain, 2006; Reilley, 2005). College counselors will vary widely in their training and expertise to make such assessments, and oftentimes students will be referred to other professionals both on and off campus for this purpose. It is common for ADHD to be underdiagnosed, misdiagnosed, or erroneously self-diagnosed by students (Reilley, 2005). Part of the problem with diagnosing ADHD is that many of the symptoms are common to or coexist with other disorders, such as mood disorders, anxiety disorders, and substance abuse (Ramsay & Rostain, 2006; Reilley, 2005). There can also be medical conditions (e.g., hypothyroidism) that might contribute to ADHD symptoms (Reilley, 2005).

College counselors assist students with ADHD by providing academic counseling, teaching techniques to improve coping skills, and providing counseling for coexisting problems such as anxiety and depression. College counselors can also be involved in ensuring that students acquire and use medication appropriately and utilize available support services and accommodations (Javorsky & Gussin, 1994). One form of treatment that has been found to be particularly promising for helping students with ADHD is cognitive-behavioral therapy (CBT) (Ramsay & Rostain, 2006). This form of therapy focuses on establishing specific behavioral goals and changing negative, self-defeating thought patterns. CBT can also help students come to terms with the ADHD diagnosis and the fact that students with ADHD need to extend themselves harder to make it through college (Ramsay & Rostain, 2006).

Assisting Students With Autism Spectrum Disorders

Individuals diagnosed with autism spectrum disorders (ASDs) represent another growing subgroup of students with special needs on today's campuses (Farrell, 2004; Welkowitz & Baker, 2005). In general, students with these disorders who are able to attend college tend to be at the milder, high-functioning end of the spectrum (Browning & Miron, 2007). As with students with LDs and ADHD, students with ASDs (namely, Asperger's syndrome) will often be assisted by campus personnel primarily devoted to students with disabilities. However, these students are highly likely to be referred to campus counselors at some point during their time in college.

Students with ASDs are known to experience struggles in navigating the social demands of the campus environment (Browning & Miron, 2007). Because of deficiencies in social and interpersonal skills, for example, not being able to pick up on common social cues, these students are likely to experience an assortment of unintentional problems in their interactions with others. It may not be unusual for such students to elicit concern from others, including faculty and staff, who may then encourage them to seek counseling. The following case is an example of such a situation.

A female student with Asperger's (diagnosed in childhood) was referred to the counseling center by faculty members in her program. The student was enrolled in a program to prepare her for a career in elementary school teaching, and apparently there were concerns among faculty members in the department about the student's tendency to occasionally behave in ways that they perceived as socially odd, which could pose problems for someone pursuing a career in elementary education. For her to remain in the program, the faculty more or less required her to seek counseling. Interestingly, however, they never sought verification of her attendance in counseling or any specific input from the counselor about the student's problems.

The student had difficulties with simple conversation and specific nonverbal behaviors (e.g., she would only minimally avert her eye gaze, resulting in uncomfortable staring). She also had some difficulty with picking up on social cues; for example, she was known to place unreasonable demands on faculty members' time and did not have a sense of when it was time to leave their offices (unless explicitly told she needed to leave). It was not hard to imagine how others on campus, be it faculty members or fellow students, would perceive her as somewhat odd and socially awkward. However, her behavior seemed to fall within the expected norms for someone with a mild form of autism. She had an understanding of why she was referred by her program faculty and an awareness of some but not all of her social skill deficiencies.

For most college counselors, this type of case poses challenges in the sense that it requires a very different set of expectations and skills for how to do counseling. As Browning and Miron (2007) described, students with Asperger's need to be taught practical skills, such as how to engage in simple conversation, how to initiate and finish a conversation, how to behave appropriately in classroom and other settings, and how to communicate nonverbally and interpret the nonverbal behavior of others such as body language. These skills are ideally taught and tested in a supportive group setting, but they can be the focus of individual counseling as well.

Contributing to Student Retention

One of the many ways for college counselors to support the educational mission of their colleges and universities is to demonstrate that their services have a positive influence on retention. Contributing to retention efforts can take many forms. For example, centers can contribute specifically to retention efforts by having staff members participate in new student orientation, serve on campus committees related to retention, provide specialized intervention for at-risk students, and provide workshops on topics geared toward retention.

Although the primary activity of college counselors, individual counseling, is not directly or specifically aimed at retention as the goal, it has nonetheless been demonstrated to have a positive influence on retention. A review of studies on the relationship between college counseling and student retention (Sharkin, 2004b) demonstrates that counseling has a positive impact on retention regardless of whether counseling is aimed at retention-related concerns, primarily focused on academic concerns, or mostly for psychological concerns. For example, Turner and Berry (2000) found that students who received counseling for psychological concerns, on average, had a higher retention rate (85%) compared with the general student body (74%). Other studies (e.g., Bray, Braxton, & Sullivan, 1999) have shown that emotional and social adjustment difficulties, particularly for first-year students, tend to predict attrition as well as or better than academic adjustment difficulties. Although not a direct link, studies such as these suggest that the interventions of college counselors focused on the social and psychological needs of students can play a key role in retention. Indeed, a more recent study by D. Lee, Olson, Locke, Michelson, and Odes (2009) found that being in counseling was significantly related to continued enrollment in a large sample of first-year and transfer students.

It can be important to ask students directly about the influence of counseling on their academic life, particularly whether counseling plays a role in their remaining in school. In a recent survey of counseling centers (Gallagher, 2010), a majority indicated that they now ask students if their counseling experience helped them remain enrolled in school and whether counseling helped them with their academic performance. Results of these questions posed to students show that a significant percentage of them believed that counseling was instrumental in both their staying in school (59%) and enhancing their academic performance (60%).

Although it behooves college counselors to produce retention-based data as a way to demonstrate to administrators the value of their services, they should be cautious about the use of retention data as the only means of assessing college counseling effectiveness. The primary reason for this is that the goal of counseling cannot be to retain students. In other words, for counseling to be effective, counselors need to maintain a relatively neutral stance regarding students' decisions about remaining in school versus leaving school in order for students to fully explore all aspects of their decisions without any undue pressure. The last thing a counselor wants to do is try to persuade students to stay enrolled or not transfer when that is not necessarily in their best interest. College counselors can feel reassured that despite having to practice in this neutral manner, the evidence seems to strongly support the effect of counseling on retaining students. Perhaps the less counselors impose any pressure on their clients to stay enrolled, the more likely they will.

Because of the importance of demonstrating how counseling contributes to retention, college counseling centers should seriously consider offering and promoting academic counseling, if they do not already do so. Despite the fact that both forms of counseling (academic and psychological) can have positive effects on retention, academic counseling is generally perceived as more directly related to retention. Thus, doing academic counseling is likely to please administrators who appreciate activities on campus that have retention in mind as a specific goal. As noted in Chapter 2, academic counseling may share much in common with academic support services elsewhere on a campus, so it is important for college counselors to coordinate or collaborate with others to avoid duplicating services and to avoid unnecessary competition between counseling services and other departments.

Serving on Campus-Based Teams for Behavioral Intervention, Threat Assessment, and Crisis Response

Over the past several years, colleges and universities across the country began to establish teams consisting of various campus representatives designated to identify and intervene with at-risk, disruptive, and potentially violent students. The task of identifying and responding to potential threats of violence has assumed greater importance following what happened at Virginia Tech in 2007. Teams are also created for the purpose of providing a coordinated response during and after crises or traumas that occur on or near campus. College counselors are almost always participants on or consultants to these teams, based on their expertise with forms of psychological disturbance and distress such as suicidal behavior. College counselors also typically possess excellent skills for responding to crisis situations given their knowledge and understanding of acute post-traumatic stress reactions (Utterback & Caldwell, 1989).

Despite similar agendas, coordinated response teams designed for prevention can have many different titles. Examples of titles include Early Alert, Early Intervention, Risk Management, Behavioral Intervention, Student Assessment, and Threat Assessment. Teams aimed at responding to crisis situations typically have names such as Crisis Response, Emergency Response, Trauma Response, and Critical Incident Management. The risk-assessment-type teams will typically meet on a regular basis (perhaps weekly) and as needed, whereas crisis response teams will primarily convene immediately following the crisis event.

In addition to college counselors, other team members will usually come from student services administration, health services, residential life, campus police, judicial affairs, academic affairs (e.g., academic deans and faculty), and disability services. Members of the community may be represented on crisis response teams. One person will be designated as chair of the team, often the dean of students or other administrator who has the authority to implement team recommendations and has direct access to legal counsel. The team will ultimately report to a senior-level administrator such as the vice president for student services or provost. Teams will have clear policies and procedures in place for their particular purpose. Team members need to be cognizant of appropriate laws and policies regarding confidentiality and student rights. Coordinated risk assessment teams must ensure that members of the campus community are well informed about what should be reported (e.g., a student behaving strangely, a student making threats, etc.) and how to make such a report to the team. Information of this nature can be disseminated through presentations, brochures, mass e-mail, and websites.

This section will be divided into three different types of teams: Behavioral Intervention, Threat Assessment, and Crisis Response. There can be considerable overlap with the first two types of teams, given their mission of risk assessment, but it is important to devote attention to some of the unique aspects of threat assessment apart from the more general task of risk assessment.

Behavioral Intervention

A Behavioral Intervention Team (BIT) is generally established for the purpose of identifying students deemed at risk or disruptive in some way within the campus community. The most common scenarios will involve students who arouse concern because of suicide risk, intimidating or threatening behavior toward others, disruptive behavior in class or a residence hall, troublesome interactions with faculty and staff, written assignments for class or e-mail to professors that contain content interpreted as either suicidal or threatening in nature, and strange or unusual behavior. Teams aimed at intervening with students showing signs of personal troubles as soon as they are observed, even if not considered serious yet, are particularly common at smaller institutions (Wasley, 2007). Smaller campus communities, compared with larger campuses, are perhaps better able to monitor and then intervene when problems first emerge. Troubled or problematic students may more easily "fall through the cracks" at larger institutions.

Once a student is identified to the BIT, the team needs to evaluate and further investigate the information obtained about the student. Intervention can occur in several different realms (medical, psychological, judicial, and legal) and must balance the best interests of the student against the best interests of the campus community. The participation of a college counselor on a BIT is pivotal in terms of providing a mental health professional's perspective. College counselors do need to be careful, however, not to knowingly or inadvertently violate confidentiality when the student of concern is a current or former client. College counselors may experience pressures from others on campus to breach confidentiality (Gilbert, 1989; May, 2000; Sharkin, 1995), and this will be especially true when participating on a BIT.

Disruptive behavior by a student in the campus environment, whether in class or in a residence hall, can be particularly distressing to others and is a common indicator of emotional disturbance (Amada, 1992; Sharkin, 2006). College counselors have long played a significant role in helping to manage disruptive students, particularly by serving as consultants to administrators, faculty, and staff (Amada, 1992, 1993, 1994, 1997; Hernandez & Fister, 2001; Lamb, 1992). This consultative role regarding disruptive students is one of the key ways that college counselors can contribute to a BIT.

Things can become more complicated, however, if the BIT wants to have students undergo mandated psychological assessments and/or mandated counseling. Mandated assessments are used to ensure that at-risk students are evaluated by a mental health professional. Administrators who arrange mandated assessments, whether with campus counselors or with off-campus professionals, generally seek a professional's opinion as to the degree of risk in order to determine whether a student can be cleared to resume attending classes or return to a residence hall. Mandated counseling involves an explicit requirement for a student to attend counseling (on or off campus) for some specified period of time as a condition of his or her continued enrollment.

Not all college counselors see eye to eye on the issue of mandated assessments and mandated counseling. There are college counselors who will see mandated referrals, but some argue against seeing any mandated students, for example, because of concerns that it is unethical. Given the conflicting opinions of college counselors about mandated interventions and the general controversy surrounding this issue, it will be explored in more detail in Chapter 6. For now, the reader should bear in mind that the practice in which administrators and judicial affairs officers mandate students to undergo assessments and/or counseling is not uncommon and can pose challenges when college counselors either reluctantly agree or resist outright the pressures to participate in this practice.

After students are assessed or evaluated, possible BIT outcomes include allowing students to remain enrolled with no restrictions or remain enrolled under specific conditions or expectations set forth by the BIT. The latter outcome is oftentimes based on a determination of student misconduct requiring disciplinary consequences. The most serious outcome would be an involuntary withdrawal with no possibility for reentry, but involuntary withdrawals are more often deemed temporary with specified conditions for readmission. Because there have been a number of complaints filed with the Office of Civil Rights in recent years regarding university policies on involuntary or mandatory leave (Appelbaum, 2006), it is critical for schools to have clear, well-defined policies in place and use procedures that do not infringe on students' due process rights (Coll, 1991; Dannells & Stuber, 1992; DiScala, Olswang, & Niccolls, 1992; Leach & Sewell, 1986). As with other administrative and disciplinary decisions, college counselors need to be careful not to be directly involved in involuntary withdrawal decisions (Gilbert, 1989), which is why some college counselors are concerned about doing mandated assessments (i.e., when they can result in such outcomes).

Even when an institution has a BIT in place, this does not necessarily mean that every case involving a student of concern will be addressed with a positive outcome. In addition to the lawsuits related to the shootings, Virginia Tech is also involved in a negligence lawsuit filed by the parents of a student, Daniel Kim, who committed suicide later the same year of the shootings (December 2007). According to reports, Kim experienced distress after the campus shootings, largely because he believed he resembled Seung-Hui Cho and felt ashamed of his Korean ancestry (Sturgeon, 2009).

This was an unfortunate case in which the student came to the attention of a campus-based intervention team (called the CARE team) that included the director of counseling and assistant director of psychiatric services. According to the lawsuit, the team read and discussed an e-mail message from a friend of Kim's (who attended another university) that expressed serious concern about Kim being suicidal; the team chose to have local police conduct a welfare check on him, at which time he denied being suicidal, and no further action was taken. Kim was not contacted by anyone on the CARE team, and he was not evaluated by a mental health professional, even though the CARE team's protocol for students potentially at risk for suicide requires someone on the team to have contact with the on-call psychologist. About a month later, the student was found dead from a self-inflicted gunshot wound. The lawsuit claims that the CARE team failed to respond appropriately once it received information about Kim's risk for suicide and instead relied on the observations of an "untrained" police officer. This case is a sobering reminder that any intervention team established for the purpose of ensuring student safety should have and follow procedures for students to be properly evaluated by mental health professionals, particularly in cases of suicidal risk. Teams devoted to concerns related to students being at risk for harm to others will be addressed in the next section.

Threat Assessment

The task of conducting threat assessment and response will sometimes come under the purview of a BIT, but some campuses now have teams specifically designated for the purpose of threat assessment. Although the Virginia Tech tragedy led to a nationwide surge in protocols and coordinated efforts for doing threat assessment (Cornell, 2008), it is not as if violent crime did not exist before that on college campuses. In fact, it was the 1986 case of Jeanne Clery, a 19-year-old student who was raped and murdered in her residence hall at Lehigh University, that prompted enactment of the Crime Awareness and Campus Security Act of 1990, later renamed the Jeanne Clery Disclosure of Campus Security Policy and Crime Statistics Act (Hunter & Lowery, 2008). The parents of Jeanne Clery lobbied Congress to enact legislation that would help ensure campus safety. The law requires institutions of higher education to publish annual crime statistics, keep public crime logs, and provide timely warnings about safety (Hunter & Lowery, 2008).

Despite the notoriety of high-profile incidents that garner national media attention and create a heightened sense of danger, college campuses have traditionally been relatively safe environments with low rates of violent crime (Cornell, 2008). College students are actually more likely to be victims of violent crime off campus than on campus; 93% of crimes experienced by students occur off campus (Cornell, 2008). However, according to a recent report issued by the FBI, Secret Service, and Department of Education, cases of campus violence have increased over the past two decades (Yost, 2010). These statistics include cases involving employees as well as current and former students and pertain to situations in which attackers select a victim beforehand or randomly select victims based on some predetermined profile or relationship. Some cases of campus-related violence involve acts of violence perpetrated by nonstudents against students or vice versa; for example, in a recent incident at Youngstown (Ohio) State University, two nonstudents were accused of spraying bullets into a fraternity house party, killing one student and injuring several others, allegedly after they had been ejected from the party.

The increase in violent crime may be related, in part, to an increase in the possession of weapons on campus. An increase in weapons-related arrests on campuses was observed a number of years ago (Lederman, 1994). Acts of campus violence, which are mostly committed by males (over 90%), oftentimes involve firearms (over 50%) (Yost, 2010). Possession of firearms on campus, which can be as high as 3% to 5% of the student population based on some estimates (Meilman, Leichliter, & Presley, 1998; M. Miller, Hemenway, & Wechsler, 2002), tend to be highest among binge-drinking males who engage in aggressive and dangerous behavior after drinking (M. Miller et al., 2002). Because it is generally students with weapons who pose the primary concern, the recent case of a professor killing three colleagues during a faculty meeting at the University of Alabama at Huntsville was quite shocking and reminded us that violent crime on campus is not limited to students.

Other forms of violence encountered on campuses are hate crimes (Downey & Stage, 1999), stalking, cyberstalking, bullying, cyberbullying, relationship violence, and sexual assault and rape (Paludi, 2008). Female students may be particularly concerned about their personal safety on campus (B. T. Kelly & Torres, 2006). Such safety concerns of female students are currently receiving national attention as officials of the Department of Education's Office for Civil Rights are investigating complaints by 16 female students at Yale University that the university has repeatedly failed to adequately respond to reports of harassment, rape, attempted rape, and stalking (Christoffersen, 2011). Female students may also be vulnerable to relationship violence. The murder of Yeardley Love at the University of Virginia in 2010 has brought increased awareness and attention to the specific problem of relationship violence among college students (Wertheim, 2010). Love's former boyfriend, George Huguely, was charged with her murder, though he claims that her death was an accident. After the murder, reports began to emerge suggesting that Huguely had a history of violent behavior associated with alcohol abuse.

Although some concerns (e.g., sexual harassment) may be reported to specific administrative staff or offices designated to address such concerns, any concerns involving potential threats of harm within the campus community can be brought to the attention of a Threat Assessment Team (TAT). The process of threat assessment typically consists of an evaluation of a threat and determination of the likelihood of it being carried out. Hence, once a TAT is informed of a potential threat situation, it will investigate whether a student has the intent and means to carry out the threat and will do whatever is possible to prevent any intended threat from posing a danger to specific individuals or the campus community. A TAT will rely on clear, systematic procedures for evaluating the level of risk. For example, some teams may use a risk rubric to classify threats, such as the one developed by the National Center for Higher Education Risk Management (2010), which classifies degree of risk from low to extreme. The TAT has to make a judgment about whether there is need for immediate action or if a student can be referred for an evaluation.

A specific case that illustrates how a TAT may get called on occurred at Millersville University (Pennsylvania) in March 2008. Although there may not actually have been a TAT involved in this case, one can easily imagine how the use of a TAT would have been appropriate. According to news reports, 24-year-old student Joel Yodis became angry when classmates laughed at him, and he then reportedly used his hand to imitate the firing of a gun. This, of course, was deemed as a threat. One of the students notified a professor via e-mail and apparently expressed concern that Yodis may have possessed a gun. The concerned student indicated being afraid to attend class with Yodis for fear of being harmed. As a result, Public Safety placed the campus on lockdown for nearly two hours until the student was eventually found in the campus library.

Because this incident occurred just about a year after the Virginia Tech shootings, it may seem like a case of overreaction based on the heightened anxieties on campuses at that time. Nevertheless, any threatening gesture that is reported must be taken seriously and carefully investigated. The action of a TAT in a case such as this might very well have come to the same result, or perhaps there would have been a call to locate the student and have him evaluated without initiating a campus lockdown. If an event like this had occurred 20 years ago, it might not have even triggered any type of report, let alone a lockdown. But these are the times in which we now live. The student was subsequently charged with making terroristic threats; he pled no contest and was given 3 years of probation.

Because of concerns about the growing role of college counselors in threat assessment, this topic will be revisited in Chapter 6. Specifically, the unique challenges for college counselors associated with their involvement in threat assessment, whether as part of a TAT or through mandated assessments, will be the subject of further discussion.

Crisis Response

Whereas a BIT or TAT is aimed at *prevention* of crisis situations or acts of violence, a Crisis Response Team (CRT) is usually mobilized to manage and respond to crises or traumatic events that actually occur. The primary task of a CRT is to help students and the campus community cope in the aftermath of a crisis or critical incident occurring on or near campus. Examples of crisis events include unexpected student death(s), violent crime and murder, completed suicides, accidents and fires, and medical-related crises (such as cases of meningitis). The specific tasks will vary depending on the type of incident but typically entail providing accurate information about the incident, helping to manage acute and post-traumatic stress reactions, providing reassurance, helping to manage fears and contain panic, and ensuring the well-being of the campus community (Casey, 2004; Eaves, 2001; Roth, Reed, & Donnelly, 2005; Wiesen & Lischer, 2006). It is particularly important for the CRT to help the campus heal and gradually return to normalcy (Schwitzer, 2003). A number of interventions can be provided or arranged by the CRT such as debriefings, on-scene interventions, and emergency counseling, depending on the specific incident (Casey, 2004).

Events that take place off campus can be traumatic to a campus as well. A prime example is the serial murders of five University of Florida students in their off-campus apartments in 1990 (Archer, 1992). The murders resulted in heightened anxieties, as many students chose to leave campus until the killer was caught. There was a tremendous need for crisis management and rumor control to contain widespread fear and panic (Archer, 1992). Natural disasters such as tornadoes and earthquakes that occur on or near campus will often require a crisis response (McCarthy & Butler, 2003). For example, a tornado that occurred at the University of Maryland on September 24, 2001, resulted in the death of two students, numerous injuries, and damage to several buildings. Even larger scale events that affect the whole country, such as the September 11th terrorist attacks, may call for campus intervention (Cardenas, Williams, Wilson, Fanouraki, & Singh, 2003; DeRoma et al., 2003), especially on campuses closest to the event (e.g., NYU) during the terror attacks (Dale & Alpert, 2006).

When traumatic events, such as murder, occur on or near campus, the CRT will need to be prepared to deal with the media. As counseling center directors, Archer (1992) and Stone (1993) gave personal accounts that included having to handle the media during highly publicized multiple murders of students (at the University of Florida) and university personnel (at the University of Iowa in 1991), respectively. In particular, Archer spoke about the challenge of controlling rumors that were generating more fear and panic throughout the campus. In such situations when college counselors are asked to respond to the media, they typically work closely with the school's public or media relations office.

Serving on University Committees and Task Forces

College counselors are often involved in university governance through participation on committees and task forces. Committee work is an essential component of institutions of higher education. Colleges and universities rely on committees and appointed task forces to address and make recommendations on important matters pertaining to administration, budget, curriculum, new programs, policies, strategic goals and action plans, health and safety, personnel, and campus life. Of course, college counselors will generally be involved in any committee work related to student mental health, but they can and do contribute to an array of committees that have other agendas. College counselors participate on committees originating within their division (most commonly student affairs or student services) as well as campus-wide committees. Counseling center directors will often have specific committees that they need to attend, such as regular meetings of all division directors.

College counselors are considered to possess excellent skills for membership on committees and may be especially equipped to be effective as leaders or chairpersons on committees (Parr, Jones, & Bradley, 2006). This is because college counselors typically possess knowledge and expertise about group dynamics and process. Committees can be conceptualized as a type of group, in most instances a task group with a specific purpose. The experience that college counselors acquire from facilitating counseling groups can certainly be applicable when serving as a member of a committee and especially when serving as chair of a committee (Parr et al., 2006).

An example of the type of committee that a college counselor might serve on would be one that is established to address matters of campus climate. Most campuses have a committee of this nature designed to address a variety of issues and concerns, such as promoting increased understanding of and sensitivity to issues of diversity, social justice, and equity on campus. Any specific areas of concern can be raised by such a committee, which can then develop recommendations for addressing the concerns. College counselors can make significant contributions to committees such as this, given their unique knowledge and skills in matters critical to the campus life and culture, for example, the promotion of sensitivity to diversity on one's campus (which will be addressed in Chapter 5).

One of the advantages of committee work is the collaboration with faculty and staff members from other departments. Committee work represents an ideal way to work with others, which can result in even further joint efforts, such as the planning and cosponsoring of campus events and programs, research projects, and other ventures. In addition to some of the departments with whom college counselors commonly collaborate that have already been mentioned (e.g., Health Services, Residential Life, Public Safety, and Judicial Affairs) are Athletics, International Students' Office, Women's Center, Multicultural Services, and Financial Aid. It is often through committee involvement that these relationships are enhanced and strengthened, allowing for more opportunities to find additional ways to work together for the betterment of students and the campus community.

Teaching

Little has been written about college counselors as educators, but this is certainly another significant contribution that many college counselors make on their campuses. Some college counselors may actually hold joint appointments whereby they spend half of their time in the counseling center and the other half teaching and performing other duties in an academic department. Whether this type of arrangement is truly 50–50 is debatable, as one can easily imagine the challenges of managing such a joint appointment. Perhaps the most common arrangement is for a college counselor to hold adjunct instructor status in a psychology, counseling, or counseling-related academic program housed on his or her campus. College counselors can also serve as adjunct instructors at other institutions. Adjunct or affiliate status can consist of more than just teaching, for instance, serving on graduate student thesis or dissertation committees, but teaching will be the primary role for most adjunct faculty members. Even when not holding adjunct status, many college counselors are asked to present guest lectures to students on various subjects.

A college counselor's eligibility to teach may depend on his or her degree, as many undergraduate and graduate programs require instructors to have doctoral degrees. As far as what courses college counselors can teach, the possibilities are contingent on the individual's specific educational background, training experiences, and areas of expertise. Some examples of courses that college counselors may teach include theories and principles of counseling, helping skills, group counseling, family counseling, ethical issues, standardized tests and measurement, career development, and counseling practicum. Counselors will teach courses for which they are qualified to teach.

Students can really benefit from instructors who can incorporate actual clinical examples in their instruction. As practitioners, college counselors have interesting case material they can share with students when teaching concepts of counseling and therapy. Of course, college counselors need to adhere to ethical principles associated with the sharing of case material for educational purposes. This is generally a matter of concealing any identifying information of clients and altering some of the demographics or other information that might inadvertently reveal the identity of the client.

One issue that deserves mention here is the potential for dual-role complications to occasionally emerge when college counselors choose to teach. Ethical codes are clear that one should never have the two roles of teaching and counseling concurrently with any students. However, some situations are awkward but not necessarily unethical. For example, it would not be unusual for counselors who also teach either to have former clients enroll in their class or to have former students eventually seek counseling with them. In most instances, these situations can be managed without any problem. The former situation (of a former client as a student in class) is perhaps somewhat more awkward, especially depending on the extent and nature of the counseling work with the student.

Similar dilemmas can arise in the context of training and supervision: A former client of the counseling center subsequently seeks a training experience in the center, or a former trainee subsequently seeks treatment. Again, these situations can often occur with few or no issues, but some counseling centers may have policies in place to try to minimize these types of situations. For example, some centers may institute a policy that restricts graduate students in the university's academic counseling program from pursuing both training and counseling in the center. In other words, if they participate in a practicum in the center, they will no longer be eligible for counseling services and vice versa. Such policies need to be disseminated to all students in the counseling program so that they can make this decision as early as needed. Of course, for those students who become ineligible for counseling on campus, off-campus referrals should be provided.

Summary

In addition to the primary roles described in Chapter 2 (i.e., counseling, crisis intervention, outreach, etc.), college counselors contribute in other vital ways to the educational mission of their universities. College counselors assist students with academic-related matters and decisions, learning disorders, attention deficit problems, and autism-related problems. The services that college counselors provide to students have been shown to have a positive impact on student retention. College counselors also make significant contributions to their institutions by serving on important committees, including but not limited to committees devoted to behavioral intervention, threat assessment, and crisis response. Many college counselors also serve as instructors of courses at the undergraduate and graduate levels and may play key roles as affiliates of academic programs on their campuses.

4

PROFESSIONAL ACTIVITIES
OF COLLEGE COUNSELORS

As professionals in counseling, psychology, social work, and other related fields, college counselors engage in a number of professional activities. Some of these activities may lie outside the scope of their work on campus, but many of them are related to their counseling center duties. In fact, for many college counselors, professional activities (such as acquiring and maintaining licensure) may be a requirement for continued employment, whereas other activities (such as research productivity and involvement in professional organizations) may not necessarily be required but are encouraged or expected to some extent. This chapter will delve into the following professional activities of college counselors: research and scholarly work, membership and involvement in professional organizations, licensure and certification, continuing education and professional development, and private practice.

Research and Scholarly Work

Research is viewed as an integral component of a college counseling center that can enhance counseling services (Bishop, Gallagher, & Cohen, 2000; Boyd et al., 2003). Research can be in the form of ongoing evaluation of the effectiveness of programs and services, studies on student characteristics and development, and any project or scholarly endeavor that advances professional knowledge in one's field. At the very least, college counselors need to be able to understand and make use of current studies in their professional practice, particularly if they want to maintain an evidence-based approach to practice that relies on empirically supported treatments (Cooper, 2005). This would require that they read journal articles and keep abreast of the most current research. The *Journal of College Counseling*, the *Journal of College Student Psychotherapy*, and the *Journal of College Student Development* are three prominent outlets for research that is especially relevant to college counseling. College counselors serve as editorial board members and ad hoc reviewers for these and similar scholarly journals.

Despite the importance of research and scholarly work in college counseling, it has tended to be viewed as lower in priority than other functions, especially when compared to the provision of counseling services. Cooper and Archer (2002) conducted a survey of counseling center directors and found that research was not high on the list of center priorities and that research productivity was relatively low. The relative dearth of research productivity among college counselors has been attributed to a variety of reasons, such as the fact that they are generally more practice oriented, have little time to conduct research, and tend not to receive "rewards" (such as tenure and promotion) for doing research (Bishop et al., 2000; Cooper & Archer, 2002; Phelps, 1992). They did find, however, that research for evaluation and accountability purposes was done with more frequency. Although not necessarily conducted with the scientific rigor generally associated with publishable research, more practical research that is used for annual reports, demonstration of the effectiveness of counseling services, and justification for increased funding or staffing can be quite valuable.

For some college counselors, doing research is simply part of their professional identity. Many college counselors were trained in the *scientist–practitioner model*, first adopted as a training model for professional psychology many years ago (Mellott, 2007). This model conceptualizes science and practice as not only inseparable but interdependent: Practice inspires research questions, and research informs practice. Hence, to be true scientist-practitioners, individuals need to balance and integrate the two into their professional lives.

Barnette (2006) described how the scientist-practitioner model has strongly influenced her professional identity as a college counselor. She suggested that college counseling centers are ideal settings for those who wish to aspire to the model, given the variety of professional activities as well as the many opportunities for research that come with working in academic settings. Barnette is a strong proponent of working on research teams, which can be an excellent way to collaborate with professional colleagues at one's own institution as well as at other institutions and with students.

A specific form of research that has been especially critical for counseling centers over the years is the use of annual national surveys of counseling center directors conducted by Robert Gallagher at the University of Pittsburgh and by the Association of University and College Counseling Directors (AUCCCD). These surveys present data on a range of topics and concerns within the profession, such as administrative issues, budget trends, ethical dilemmas, innovations, and clinical services. Data from both surveys, which are frequently referenced in this book, can be quite helpful in allowing counseling centers to compare statistics and keep abreast of current issues in college counseling.

Another notable form of data collection that should be invaluable to college counselors is the recently established national database under the leadership of the Center for Collegiate Mental Health (CCMH) at Pennsylvania State University. This long-term collaborative project consists of data pooling among a growing list of participating counseling centers around the country (currently at more than 130) that use a similar software scheduling program. Data are based on a standardized intake instrument, the Counseling Center Assessment of Psychological Symptoms (CCMH, 2009), designed to assess various aspects of mental health of college students who seek counseling. This not only will allow counseling centers to make comparisons with national norms but will also encourage more research on college student mental health concerns.

In addition to publishing research studies in professional journals, college counselors can also present their research findings at professional conferences. These presentations can be on a local, regional, national, or international level. The format of presentations can range from simple poster sessions in which a summary of one's research is displayed for a brief period to longer paper presentations in front of an audience. Presenting research at professional gatherings and conferences represents a wonderful way for college counselors to exchange ideas with peers in the field and stay current with professional issues and innovative practices. Webinars, which can be presented at several different locations simultaneously, are becoming increasingly popular as an alternative to the traditional venue of having professionals attend a conference in one location.

Membership and Involvement in Professional Organizations

Aside from the opportunity to present research at conferences, membership in local, regional, and national professional associations provides new and practicing college counselors (as well as students) with several benefits that can enhance their professional development and identity. According to International Association of Counseling Services accreditation standards (Boyd et al., 2003), college counselors are expected to hold membership and participate in appropriate professional organizations. Professional organizations typically provide valuable resources including publications and journals, websites, and LISTSERVs, all of which help keep members current on professional issues and trends (Francis, 2000). Membership can be a key way to connect and network with others in the field all across the country. In addition, there are opportunities to become involved in the organization's governance and leadership by serving on committees or holding office.

Most, if not all, college counselors will retain membership in one or more professional organizations. Because of the diversity in their educational and training backgrounds, college counselors will vary in the number and type of organizations to which they belong. College counselors who have a counseling background may choose to be members of the American Counseling Association (ACA), whereas those who are psychologists may choose to be members of the American Psychological Association (APA). There are also organizations for other types of professionals, such as social workers (National Association of Social Workers) and mental health counselors (American Mental Health Counselors Association). These large organizations typically consist of smaller associations or divisions (and sections within the divisions) representing specific specialties or areas of interest. Within ACA, for example, there is the division of the American College Counseling Association (ACCA).

ACCA is a highly regarded and especially relevant association for college counselors. It is devoted to and supports the practice of college counseling, promotes ethical practices, provides advocacy for the profession, and promotes networking among college counselors nationwide. The division publishes what is perhaps now the preeminent journal for college counselors, the *Journal of College Counseling*. The association also holds annual conferences that provide continuing education opportunities and bring together thousands of college counselors from around the country. Similar to ACA, a division within APA (the Society of Counseling Psychology) contains a section specifically devoted to counseling center practitioners. Another valuable organization for college counselors is the American College Personnel Association, which includes the Commission for Counseling and Psychological Services.

Other important organizations include the Association of Counseling Center Training Agencies (for counseling center training directors) and the Association of Psychology Postdoctoral and Internship Centers (for counseling centers that are accredited as predoctoral internship sites and postdoctoral residency programs). Of particular interest to counseling center directors is AUCCCD. This association, established in 1950, brings together counseling center directors from colleges throughout the United States, Canada, Europe, and Asia. According to its mission statement, the association is devoted to the awareness of college student mental health issues through research, advocacy, education, and training. Membership in AUCCCD is institutional and limited to institutions that offer bachelor and/or graduate degrees. A number of counseling center directors may also get involved in the National Association of Student Personnel Administrators, which includes administrators in all components of student affairs and student services.

Licensure and Certification

Most college counselors pursue licensure in the state in which they practice. *Licensure* is a government-regulated credential that exemplifies competence to practice based on specific state-determined educational qualifications, supervised clinical experience, and the passing of a national exam. Licensure is designed to protect the public and ensure a certain level of training and expertise. Most states require the passing of oral and/or written exams pertaining to state laws and regulations and/or other areas of professional practice. Laws for licensure generally govern both the use of a title (e.g., "psychologist") and the scope of practice. Licensure is necessary for an individual to practice independently and be eligible for reimbursement from third-party and private payers. Common types of licensed college counselors are licensed professional counselors and licensed psychologists.

Some college counselors will also pursue certification from professional certification organizations. *Certification* means that an individual has fulfilled a set of qualifications and standards determined by a professional organization giving her or him recognition of expertise and competence in a specialty area and use of a specific title (e.g., national certified counselor or NCC). Many practitioners seek certification for purposes of enhancing their professional identity as well as promoting their special skills. Being licensed for a specified period of time is often a prerequisite for eligibility for certification. As an example, a psychologist who has been licensed for 2 years as an independent practitioner may seek specialty certification (in a specific domain such as counseling, clinical, or school psychology) by applying to the American Board of Professional Psychology. Psychologists can also apply to be listed in the National Register of Health Service Providers, which is especially helpful for those in private practice who want to be recognized by insurance companies. A counselor can become board certified (as an NCC) by meeting the requirements of the National Board for Certified Counselors.

Much has been written about professional credentialing of counselors and psychologists (Bradley, 1995; Brooks, 1996; Hosie, 1995; Kaslow & Echols, 2006; Munley, Duncan, McDonnell, & Sauer, 2004; Pate, 1995; Tarvydas & Hartley, 2009), and the reader is referred to these other sources for more in-depth discussions. Whether current or eventual licensure is required for a college counseling center position is usually dependent on the particular center and its specific needs. For example, centers that provide training and supervision to trainees may need staff members to be licensed in order to meet supervision requirements. Certification, on the other hand, is generally sought voluntarily and is not required for employment in college counseling centers. One form of certification that will sometimes be required is certification in addictions or substance abuse counseling for a substance abuse specialist position. There are several different types of certification in addictions counseling (Mustaine, West, & Wyrick, 2003; Page & Bailey, 1995), with the "certified addictions counselor" bestowed by the International Certification Reciprocity Consortium being perhaps the most common among counseling center addictions specialists.

Continuing Education and Professional Development

Ongoing professional development activities are considered essential for those that work in college counseling (Boyd et al., 2003). In fact, once licensed, college counselors are required to participate in continuing education (CE) and other forms of professional development in order to retain their license to practice. Most states now have mandated CE requirements for all types of licensure. States require CE to ensure that practitioners maintain competence, keep abreast of new developments in their field, and provide high-quality services. Although mandated to do so, practitioners tend to be oriented toward engaging in professional development activities in order to enhance their skills and clinical effectiveness. Attending CE programs is also a way for clinicians of all types to network and socialize. Attendance at presentations and programs at professional conferences can qualify for CE credits. In addition, some in-service programs can qualify if they have appropriate approval and sponsorship. In some states, CE credits can be earned by teaching undergraduate and graduate courses, presenting papers at conferences, and publishing research. There are also home study courses available for earning credits. There can be restrictions, however, on the amount of credit that can be earned from any one source.

In terms of attendance at programs, college counselors will typically try to attend programs that have relevance to their work with the college student population. The range of subjects is so vast that there will usually be plenty of programs to choose from. Examples include programs on specific types of disorders such as anxiety and mood disorders, personality disorders, and substance abuse. Even if not aimed at college students per se, these types of programs can be quite applicable and relevant for college counseling work. Programs on specific forms of assessment and treatment, psychopharmacology, and ethics and legal issues tend to be quite valuable as well.

With respect to continuing education, the prevailing wisdom is that one can never become complacent and assume there is nothing new to learn. This type of work, as with most other professions, is a lifelong learning process. Thus, professional development in general and the acquisition of CE credit in particular are simply part of the process of being a professional practitioner. Most professionals in college counseling are motivated to continue to learn and improve, even those who have been practicing for many years.

Private Practice

Once licensed, a number of college counselors will choose to maintain a private practice in addition to their counseling center position. It is actually not that uncommon for counseling center practitioners to choose private practice as a primary outlet if and when they resign from working in counseling centers (Wachowiak & Simono, 1996). It can be difficult to manage a full-time counseling center position and a private practice at the same time, but many opt to do it for a variety of reasons.

Aside from the challenge of maintaining a private practice while also working at a college counseling center, doing both simultaneously can pose unique ethical dilemmas. Berger et al. (2002) identified two key potential ethical conflicts that could emerge in this situation: conflict of interest and conflict of commitment. The first type of conflict occurs when the counselor's private practice is in competition with her or his employment in a college counseling center. In other words, college counselors should not use their counseling center position to recruit or gain clients. The second type of conflict concerns the potential for there to be different levels of commitment between the counselor's employer (counseling center), students, and the counselor's own interests. Questions can be raised about the counselor's objectivity and whether decisions are made in the best interests of students.

Because of the potential for ethical problems, Berger et al. (2002) drafted a set of guidelines for college counselors in private practice to use to avoid any improprieties. They enumerate, for example, the circumstances under which it would be appropriate for college counselors to see students in their private practice: when students are not currently enrolled and therefore ineligible for counseling on campus, when students have reached the limit of counseling sessions allowed on campus, when counseling is not available on campus (e.g., during summer), or when students specifically request private practice rather than campus services. The authors of these guidelines also recommend that when students need or request services off campus, they be given at least a few referrals in addition to counseling center staff members in private practice.

Summary

College counselors devote much of their time to professional activities that either are directly related to their counseling center work or lie outside of their duties on campus. These endeavors can be in the form of doing research and scholarly writing, being involved in professional associations, acquiring and maintaining licensure, seeking recognition of specific areas of expertise through certification, engaging in various types of professional development, and maintaining an independent counseling practice. Because some of these activities do not necessarily fall within the expected duties of college counselors but are pursued for the purpose of professional growth and identity, they may not be as visible to others who work within the college setting. Thus, it is important to highlight the many ways that college counselors devote themselves to their profession and make valuable contributions within their field.

5

BEING A DIVERSITY-COMPETENT COLLEGE COUNSELOR

The college student population has become increasingly diverse over the past few decades (Bishop, Lacour, Nutt, Yamada, & Lee, 2004; Cooper, Resnick, Rodolfa, & Douce, 2008; Hodges, 2001). Although institutions of higher education were once almost exclusive domains of young, White, affluent males, they have since transformed themselves to better reflect the diversity of our society. The term *diversity* used to be primarily associated with ethnicity and race, but the term has expanded to include demographic variables such as age, gender, gender identity, sexual orientation, socioeconomic status, religious affiliation, and ability status. In response to the significant changes in the student population, college counselors have recognized the need to acquire and develop appropriate skills for working with diverse groups of students.

Diversity and multicultural skills are now considered to be essential for those in the profession of college counseling (Berg-Cross & Pak, 2006; Resnick, 2006; Reynolds & Pope, 2003). Being a diversity-competent college counselor entails going beyond just individual counseling skills and truly engenders a much broader scope of activity and practice. College counselors need to be sensitive to and promote diversity in all aspects of campus life (Wright, 2000).

This chapter will begin with a discussion of how colleges and universities strive to fully embrace diversity on their campuses and what it means to be a diversity-competent college counselor. This will be followed by a discussion of how college counselors incorporate diversity into all dimensions of their work. The chapter will conclude with a brief overview of the unique struggles of diverse student groups, the importance of providing appropriate and responsive counseling to a diverse student population, and some of the ways that college counselors reach out to diverse students on campus.

Embracing Diversity

As Jenkins (1999) once observed, it is not a simple task to truly capture the essence of diversity, as reflected, for example, in our struggles over the years to find adequate terms for diverse populations: *disenfranchised*, *marginalized*, *underserved*, *oppressed*, *culturally different*, and *nontraditional*, to name a few. Though there may be myriad ways to define or think about diversity, the crux of diversity is primarily about acceptance, affirmation, validation, and appreciation of human differences. In an ideal world, no individual or group would ever feel excluded or marginalized because of being different or holding minority status.

When we look at where we are as a society with respect to embracing diversity, we certainly have evolved in significant ways and yet still have much more progress to achieve. In some ways, college campuses have been at the forefront as models for how to embrace diversity. There has been a tremendous effort on the part of colleges and universities to ensure that diversity is not just acknowledged but valued and celebrated. Institutions of higher education have long aspired to recruit and retain diverse staff and faculty members. It is now common for colleges to hold campus-wide diversity activities and events, such as ethnic heritage celebrations. Many campuses now have offices devoted to multicultural services as well as multicultural resource centers. You will also typically find offices and centers with specific services for women, international students, and nontraditional students. Most colleges strive hard to make all students feel accepted and supported on their campuses, with special attention deservedly devoted to underrepresented groups.

As part of the overall diversity effort on campus, college counselors do their part to promote the appreciation of diversity throughout the campus community. The diversity-competent college counselor is expected to maintain a keen awareness of and sensitivity to issues of diversity. This includes an understanding of the roles of race, culture, gender, age, sexual orientation, and other demographic factors in the emotional and psychological problems of individual students. The diversity-competent college counselor has a good understanding of cultural and societal influences that can leave students feeling oppressed, powerless, and alienated and can result in incidents of racism, racial and sexual harassment, homophobia, and other forms of intolerance. The diversity-competent college counselor is continually challenged to confront any of his or her own personal experiences and biases that might pose barriers to being able to fully embrace and promote diversity (Jenkins, 1999).

Incorporating Diversity Into All Aspects of College Counseling

In essence, virtually all of the activities and functions of college counselors described in Chapters 2, 3, and 4 can be viewed through a diversity lens. College counselors aspire to maintain a diversity or multicultural perspective when performing their duties and to practice as diversity-competent counselors in all of their duties. Much of the guidance for practicing as diversity-competent college counselors comes from clearly delineated multicultural guidelines and competencies (e.g., American Psychological Association, 2000, 2003; American Psychological Association, Office of Ethnic Minority Affairs, 1991; Arredondo et al., 1996; Roysircar, Sandhu, & Bibbins, 2003; Sue & Sue, 2003).

Several authors (Fukuyama & Delgado-Romero, 2003; Grieger & Toliver, 2001; Perez, Fukuyama, & Coleman, 2005; Resnick, 2006; Reynolds & Pope, 2003) have identified the many ways that college counselors can implement available guidelines for practicing as diversity-competent practitioners on their campuses. Although the focus is often on the need for effective or culturally sensitive counseling practices (e.g., Berg-Cross & Pak, 2006), broader recommendations for infusing diversity into all aspects of college counseling have been suggested.

Resnick (2006) described how multiculturalism can be incorporated into all dimensions of college counseling center activity, including an understanding of the cultural context of client concerns in counseling, policies and procedures, websites and publications, outreach programs, training curricula, staff development, evaluation of services, and research. Resnick also noted that the physical environment of a college counseling center should demonstrate that diversity is valued (e.g., through artwork and waiting room magazines).

Perez et al. (2005) similarly examined how multicultural guidelines could be implemented in a range of activities within the larger college

counseling center domains of counseling (e.g., implementing culturally appropriate interventions) and training curricula (e.g., multicultural seminars for trainees). Like Resnick (2006), Perez et al. argued
that change needs to occur on a systemic level such that a counseling
center is essentially transformed into a *multicultural counseling center.*
In a similar vein, Reynolds and Pope (2003) outlined how counseling centers need to establish a strategic plan with goals for becoming
multicultural, which includes everything from the mission statement
and physical environment to policy review and the recruitment and
retention of diverse staff. Such an effort may first require a center
to undergo a self-assessment, possibly using an outside consultant
(Resnick, 2006). Fukuyama and Delgado-Romero (2003) provided
an example of how multicultural competencies were incorporated into
all aspects of activity at one counseling center on a large, predominantly White campus (University of Florida).

Helping to Meet the Needs of Diverse Student Groups on Campus

Some of the more frequently identified diverse student populations
with special needs include students of color; multiracial or multiple
heritage students; international students; gay, lesbian, bisexual, transgender, or questioning (GLBTQ) students; nontraditional students;
military veterans; and students with disabilities. Although certain
generalizations have been made about the issues most commonly faced
by students in these groups, it is important to keep in mind that there
can be significant diversity within each group. In addition, students
will often identify with two or more of these groups; for example, a
gay Asian American military veteran who returns to college at age 28
after serving in the military during the war in Iraq.

Students of color include but are not limited to African American,
Asian American, Hispanic and Latino American, and Native
American students. Students of color who attend predominantly
White institutions may experience struggles associated with their race
or minority status. Issues likely to emerge include problems in social
interactions (e.g., misunderstandings), language and cultural barriers, social alienation and isolation, negative stereotypes and erroneous
assumptions based on race, discrimination, and racism (Berg-Cross

& Pak, 2006; Brinson & Kottler, 1995b; Constantine, Wilton, & Caldwell, 2003). It has also been observed that students of color commonly deal with family concerns and stressors while in college, such as being expected to fulfill family-related responsibilities in addition to academic demands (Berg-Cross & Pak, 2006).

Multiracial (or *multiple heritage*) students may be especially prone to struggles with issues of identity and trying to fit in on campus because of their multiple heritage background (Kenney, 2007; Nishimura, 1998; Paladino, 2009; Paladino & Davis, 2006). College may be the first time these students find themselves needing to explore or truly think about their multiple heritages (Paladino, 2009). This can occur simply as a result of completing various forms that ask students to identify their race without having the option of a multiracial category. There can be pressures to choose a monoracial group with which to identify, which can stir up feelings of confusion and conflict around one's identity.

International students temporarily reside in the United States for educational purposes and come from regions around the world including Asia and the Pacific Islands, Eastern and Western Europe, Latin America and the Caribbean, the Middle East, Africa, Australia and New Zealand, and Canada. Some of the common struggles of international students are culture shock, adjustment and acculturation, language and accent barriers, homesickness and loneliness, alienation and social isolation, discrimination and prejudice, academic-related adjustments and pressures, financial difficulties, and personal crises originating at home (Berg-Cross & Pak, 2006; Clark Oropeza, Fitzgibbon, & Baron, 1991; Johnson & Sandhu, 2007; Lin, 2000; Mori, 2000). A number of complications can emerge when international students are in crisis and possibly in need of hospitalization for mental health problems, such as challenges with communication with support systems, immigration and naturalization service regulations, and financial sponsorship (Clark Oropeza et al., 1991).

GLBTQ students often experience stress as a result of managing the stigma of being a sexual minority, internalized homophobia, the coming-out process, and the lack of support from parents, family members, and religious communities (Buhrke & Stabb, 1995; Zubernis & Snyder, 2007). GLBTQ students have been found to be particularly prone to depression, loneliness, and suicidal ideation (Westefeld, Maples, Buford, & Taylor, 2001). Negative attitudes toward students with minority sexual orientations can contribute to prejudice, discrimination, hostility, harassment, threats, and violence (D'Augelli, 1992, 1993; D'Augelli & Rose, 1990; Evans & Broido, 2002). GLBTQ students are frequently confronted with homophobic and heterosexist behavior within the campus community (Buhrke & Stabb, 1995; Lance, 2002; Palma & Stanley, 2002; Schreier, 1995).

Nontraditional students (sometimes referred to as adult college students, adult learners, or returning students) are typically 25 years and older and differ from traditional students in terms of life stage and daily life pressures (Hansen, 1999). These students often have to balance or manage multiple roles related to school, work, and family (Benshoff & Bundy, 2000; Gary, 2007; Hansen, 1999). Special needs of nontraditional students include child care and the need for evening hours for student services (Benshoff & Bundy, 2000). It can be difficult for these students to get involved or integrated into campus life, as many need to commute back and forth to campus and do not have the time to do much else other than attend classes.

Military veterans face challenges as they return to civilian life and transition to the role of college student. There is a long history of differing generations of returning veterans who required special assistance with the transition to college following the Second World War (Mathewson, 1946), the Vietnam War (O'Neill & Fontaine, 1973), and the Gulf War (Spaulding, Eddy, & Chandras, 1997). Colleges are now facing increasing numbers of returning veterans of the war in Iraq (Black, Westwood, & Sorsdal, 2007) and Afghanistan. Of all of the mental, physical, and social challenges for returning veterans, post-traumatic stress disorder (PTSD) represents one of the most common forms of distress likely to pose problems for veterans when they transition to being college students. PTSD consists of intrusive memories and flashbacks, outbursts of anger, distrust of authority, and psychological numbing (Black et al., 2007). If untreated, PTSD can contribute to other problems such as substance abuse and conflict in intimate relationships. In addition, veterans who have had closed-head injuries during their service may experience symptoms that negatively affect their academic performance.

Students with disabilities face a number of challenges and potential barriers within the college environment (Beecher, Rabe, & Wilder, 2004). Although disability laws help reduce the number of obstacles to accessibility on campus, it can still be quite challenging to navigate everyday aspects of campus life for students with mobility impairments (Beecher, Preece, & Roberts, 2007), visual impairments (Koch, 2007), and hearing impairments (K. L. Smith & Rush, 2007). Some of the specific challenges include getting to and from campus as well as to and from classes, seeking and arranging for appropriate academic accommodations, and finding accessible housing (on or off campus). Students with disabilities may also struggle with a sense of loneliness, isolation, and lack of belonging if they feel excluded from or unable to participate in social activities (Beecher et al., 2004, 2007). Negative reactions and perceptions of other students may leave students with disabilities feeling different from peers (Beecher et al., 2004, 2007). They may also face negative attitudes and reactions from faculty in response to their need for special accommodations (Beilke & Yssel, 1999).

The Provision of Diversity-Sensitive Counseling

It is imperative for college counselors to practice diversity-sensitive counseling as part of their core mission of providing direct service to students (Grieger & Toliver, 2001). There are multiple resources available on what constitutes competence in diversity-sensitive counseling (commonly referred to as culturally sensitive or culturally appropriate counseling) (e.g., Sue, Arredondo, & McDavis, 1992). Diversity-sensitive counseling competencies are not specific to college counseling but apply to all counseling professionals. However, the practice of diversity-sensitive counseling has been examined specifically within the context of college counseling (Berg-Cross & Pak, 2006; Perez et al., 2005; Reynolds & Pope, 2003).

Perez et al. (2005) succinctly summarized what is generally accepted as the three critical components of providing diversity-sensitive counseling. First, counselors need to have an awareness of their own personal cultural biases and potential blind spots when working with diverse clients. Second, counselors need to have an understanding of the unique needs and struggles of diverse clients. This encompasses having an understanding of the client's worldview and way of thinking and the ability to properly explore the cultural context of the client's concerns. Third, counselors need to use skills and techniques that are affirming and appropriate for diverse clients.

Berg-Cross and Pak (2006) delineated, in addition to these three key aspects of diversity-sensitive counseling, what they consider other important skills necessary for counselors to be effective with diverse clients. They suggested that counselors need to be sensitive to a client's multiple group affiliations, which include culture and ethnicity, race, age, gender, religion, and so forth. In addition, they highlighted the importance of counselors being sensitive to client reactions to them as well as their own reactions to clients based on cultural and demographic similarities or differences. Berg-Cross and Pak also said that counselors need to be able to judge when the subject of the student's diverse background (e.g., race or culture) should be explored in counseling.

Thus, for college counselors to be effective in their primary role of doing counseling, they need to be adequately prepared to address and work with the concerns of students from diverse backgrounds. This includes but is not limited to the diverse student populations identified in the previous section. Having strong basic or general counseling skills remains an essential requirement for any counselor, but college counselors now need to possess the additional knowledge and skills necessary to be responsive to the special needs and issues of an ever-increasing diverse student population. Most college counselors graduate from academic programs that help prepare them to work with people from diverse backgrounds, but continuing professional development in diversity-sensitive counseling remains essential throughout one's career.

Reaching Out: Going Beyond the Counseling Office

Being a diversity-competent college counselor often involves going beyond the traditional role of providing confidential one-on-one counseling within the safe confines of the counseling office (Grieger & Toliver, 2001; Reynolds & Pope, 2003). College counselors need to reach out in various ways to diverse groups of students, especially those who may be reluctant to seek counseling on their own. For example, there is ample research evidence that shows that counseling services on predominantly White campuses are significantly underutilized by students of color (Brinson & Kottler, 1995b; Constantine, Chen, & Ceesay, 1997; Davidson, Yakushka, & Sanford-Martens, 2004; Kearney, Draper, & Baron, 2005). The percentage of international students who use counseling on campus has similarly been found to be small (Brinson & Kottler, 1995a; Johnson & Sandhu, 2007; Lin, 2000; Mori, 2000; Nilsson, Berkel, Flores, & Lucas, 2004; Yakushko, Davidson, & Sanford-Martens, 2008). Many international students may be unfamiliar with counseling or will not consider seeking help with personal matters from people they do not know. Therefore, it is important for college counselors to proactively find ways to reach out to these and other diverse student groups that may not naturally seek out counseling for assistance or support.

As discussed in Chapter 2, outreach programming represents one way to take counseling services out into the community. To be inclusive of diverse students, college counselors must create ways to include culture-specific content or issues of diversity when conducting outreach programs such as interactive workshops on dating and relationships, how to cope with stress, and other topics. For instance, a workshop on dating could include subtopics of interracial dating, interfaith dating, and same-gender dating. In some cases, outreach programming may need to be specifically designed to address topics of particular interest to and for diverse groups of students. As an example, programs have been designed for reducing homophobia, invalidating stereotypes, and promoting a safe and empowering campus environment for GLBTQ students (Lance, 2002; Schreier, 1995). Programs such as these need not be limited to a particular group but ideally should be inclusive of all students to enhance campus-wide recognition of diversity.

There may be instances in which outreach programs are requested or proactively initiated in response to unfortunate incidents of bias that occur on campus. Sadly, as in the larger society, campuses have not been immune from incidents of hate that include acts of assault, harassment, and vandalism against individuals or groups because of race, ethnicity, religious affiliation, and sexual orientation (Downey

& Stage, 1999). When specific incidents occur, college counselors can conduct programs in classes, residence halls, and other campus locations to facilitate open discussions about race, gender, sexual orientation, and so on and to process feelings and reactions to such incidents (Grieger & Toliver, 2001). Even in the absence of any specific incidents, these types of programs can be an important way for college counselors to help make campus communities more diversity sensitive and inclusive (Reynolds & Pope, 2003).

Sometimes college counselors need to take risks and accept challenges in their efforts to promote diversity on campus. For example, consider the concept of two-faced racism described by Picca and Feagin (2007). On the basis of an analysis of a nationwide sample of written journal entries by White college students, they found that White students tend to behave one way when they are with students of color (called the *frontstage*) and a different way when in the presence of other White students (called the *backstage*). The behavior among students in the frontstage shows no indications of racist thoughts or inclinations. In contrast, behavior in the backstage is more likely to include tolerance of (sometimes due to the fear of speaking up) or participation in overt expressions of racism, such as racist comments and jokes. Although this may strike some as too controversial or explosive of a topic for discussion, it really represents an ideal opportunity to openly and honestly explore with students of varying racial backgrounds something that may be contributing to underlying racial tensions among students. In other words, this could be a way to bring out in the open an experience that tends to remain hidden and perhaps even more insidious than blatant expressions of racism or intolerance.

Another way for college counselors to bring their services to diverse student groups is to offer to facilitate discussion, support, or counseling groups that are held in locations other than the counseling center (Davidson et al., 2004). College counselors need to be flexible enough to not only offer their services in various settings on campus but also find alternatives to traditional counseling that might appeal more to diverse students. As an example, support groups for GLBTQ students could be held in a multicultural or GLBTQ resource center on campus, which would allow for less formal interactions (while still maintaining proper boundaries) in order to establish good trusting relationships with the students.

Another key aspect of being a diversity-competent college counselor is to make connections and collaborate with other offices on campus designed to serve the needs of diverse students on campus. Examples of some critical offices to connect with include those that provide multicultural services, international student services, disability services, and GLBTQ-related services. Most campuses also have a women's resource center, and some will have support services for nontraditional students. These campus resources are often the first place where students in distress make contact in an effort to seek help or support. In addition, most campuses will have a multitude of student clubs and organizations, many of which are intended to bring together diverse groups of students. Examples of diversified interest clubs one might find on a campus include Allies (for GLBTQ students and those who support GLBTQ students), Association for Non-Traditional Students in Higher Education (for students age 25 and older), Black Student Union, International Students Organization, Organization for Latino Awareness, Latino Student Association, Dominican Student Association, Muslim Students Association, Christian Student Fellowship, Jewish Culture Club, Phoenix Group (for students with disabilities), and Military Club (for veterans). It is vital for college counselors to proactively reach out to and establish connections with these student organizations as part of their overall effort to support diversity on their campuses.

Summary

Being diversity competent is considered to be an essential aspect of college counseling. College counselors contribute in many different ways to their institutions' overall effort to embrace and promote the appreciation of diversity throughout the campus community. In essence, college counselors incorporate diversity into all dimensions of their work. One of the key ways that college counselors make a difference is by reaching out to and working with diverse groups of students on their campuses.

6

SPECIAL CHALLENGES FOR COLLEGE COUNSELORS

As with most professions, college counseling is not without its share of challenges. In this chapter, some of the most pressing challenges college counselors face today will be examined. Some of these challenges have been ongoing for many years now. We do have more knowledge based on research and anecdotal evidence to help us face these challenges, though they still remain difficult to resolve.

The first challenge to be examined is one that has been and continues to be one of the greatest challenges for college counselors: the dilemma of meeting an ever-increasing demand for services with limited resources. Challenges associated with the need for college counselors to work within an administrative structure, particularly when dealing with adversarial or ill-informed administrators, will then be explored. This will be followed by a discussion of complications that arise from the need for college counselors to maintain confidentiality of counseling and avoid multiple relationships (whenever possible) while at the same time working collaboratively within the campus community. Three separate but interrelated issues will then be examined: anxiety that many college counselors experience in today's climate because of fears of litigation (and whether such fears are warranted), the increasing role of college counselors in threat assessment, and pressures to conduct mandated assessments and mandated counseling. This will be followed by a discussion of challenges related to new technology, such as electronic records. The chapter will conclude with a discussion of the unique challenges faced by counselors who work in community college settings.

High Demand, Limited Resources

For college counselors, the issue of increasing demand and limited resources (reflected in the mantra "doing more with less") has become like an old familiar tune. This was identified as a problem in the profession many years ago (Bishop, 1990, 1995; Stone & Archer, 1990) and remains a primary concern for counseling centers nationwide (Cooper, Resnick, Rodolfa, & Douce, 2008; Sharkin, 2006). A significant number of counseling centers have experienced reductions in their operating budgets, and some have lost clinical positions (Barr, Rando, Krylowicz, & Winfield, 2010). Many counseling center directors have identified the growing demand for services without concomitant increases in resources as a serious administrative concern (Gallagher, 2009).

The Feasibility of Imposing Session Limits

One specific strategy in response to the problem of increasing demand and limited resources is to place limits on the number of sessions allowed per student. In a survey of directors, Gallagher (2010) found that 27% of centers impose session limits and 44% promote themselves as a short-term service though without a formal session limit policy as such. In a survey by Barr et al. (2010), 48% of directors reported using session limits in their centers, though 35% do so with some flexibility. Smaller counseling centers appear to be less likely than larger centers to impose session limits (Vespia, 2007). The strategy of imposing session limits is generally used to serve a greater percentage of students and reduce the need for wait lists (Gyorky, Royalty, & Johnson, 1994). The criteria used to determine specific limits are often arbitrary, though centers will typically impose a limit somewhere in the range of 10 to 14 sessions per academic year.

Because the use of session limits or time-limited counseling has often been used as a remedy for meeting high demand for services in counseling centers, researchers have attempted to examine the effectiveness of this tactic. On the basis of a large nationwide sample of counseling centers, Draper, Jennings, Baron, Erdur, and Shankar (2002) obtained results that generally supported brief counseling (between 1 and 10 sessions) as an effective form of treatment. Other researchers (Snell, Mallinckrodt, Hill, & Lambert, 2001; Wolgast, Lambert, & Puschner, 2003; Wolgast et al., 2005) have tried to determine how many sessions are needed for most clients to show clinically significant or meaningful improvement (i.e., as indicated by a significant change in self-report measure scores of symptom distress from intake to final session). The results of these studies show that between 14 and 16 sessions are needed for 50% of clients to meet criteria for clinically significant change. However, 20 sessions may be needed for significant improvement in clients with very high levels of distress (Wolgast et al., 2005).

It is interesting to note that many students terminate counseling well before they reach the maximum allowed number of sessions (in centers with limits) (Hatchett, 2004; Uffelman & Hardin, 2002; Wolgast et al., 2005). As indicated in Chapter 2, the average number of sessions for counseling center clients tends to be about 6 (Barr et al., 2010; Gallagher, 2010; Stone, Vespia, & Kanz, 2000), whereas centers with limits generally allow for up to 10 or more sessions. Thus, it may be unnecessary to set limits in most centers given the fact that the average student will not stay in counseling for that long anyway. This is partly due to the nature of the college calendar, with its breaks and natural endpoints (i.e., end of semester, graduation, etc.). Moreover, centers that impose session limits may not necessarily serve a higher percentage of students than centers with no session limits (Gyorky et al., 1994). Even more surprising, the use of session limits can actually result in longer rather than shorter wait lists, possibly due to students expecting or feeling "entitled" to and then staying in counseling for the maximum number of sessions (Gyorky et al., 1994). Although students who voluntarily seek counseling do not necessarily have a sense about how many sessions they will need, a recent study by Owen, Smith, and Rodolfa (2009) suggested that some students may expect to receive 20 or more sessions, and this expectation can predict counseling outcome. That is, those students who expected 20 or more sessions (i.e., more than allowed) characterized counseling as less effective than students who expected less than 20.

Tryon (1995) argued that the use of session limits can actually cause more problems than if no limits are imposed and recommended finding alternative strategies such as offering biweekly sessions, reducing the length of sessions, and offering group counseling. Tryon also suggested that college counselors need to be flexible and avoid being too rigid with session limits. For example, she argued for counselors to have the latitude to see some students longer than the limit if necessary in centers with session limits. This makes sense given the individual variability in rates of improvement we tend to see among students in counseling. Simply stated, it is quite difficult to predict how many sessions are necessary for individual students. Hence, instead of imposing the same session limits for all students, it may be best to base the number of sessions on the individual student's level of symptom distress when first entering counseling (Wolgast et al., 2005). Progress in counseling can then be monitored until meaningful change or improvement is attained (Wolgast et al., 2003).

Off-Campus Referrals

Another strategy for easing the burden of high demand for services is to refer students, when appropriate, to off-campus mental health services. Students may need to be referred to off-campus resources at times when a wait list is in effect or ongoing counseling appointments are no longer available. However, off-campus referrals may be made at any point if students are not considered appropriate for campus counseling services. Simply stated, college counseling has its limitations. In fact, it has been argued that providing counseling services to students whose needs exceed typical counseling center resources can be ethically unwise and pose legal risks (Gilbert, 1992). According to ethical standards, college counselors must limit their services so as not to exceed the boundaries of their competence. Thus, students who need services beyond the scope or expertise of what a campus counseling center can reasonably provide should be referred to other services.

There are several specific criteria that counseling centers may use to determine if and when students are better served by being referred to off-campus agencies. Students who are deemed to be inappropriate for the short-term or time-limited nature of most college counseling centers may need to be referred to outside services (Lacour & Carter, 2002). This includes students who require longer term treatment for more chronic forms of mental illness or psychopathology (e.g., psycho-sis, severe personality disorder, etc.) and those who require frequent crisis and emergency intervention services. Students who need exten-sive monitoring (e.g., would need more than one session per week) or overutilize services and place an undue burden on campus counseling services are likely to be referred out.

Students who are considered high risk because they were recently hospitalized and/or are likely to require hospitalization for men-tal health issues may be referred into the community. Students who need specialized forms of treatment (e.g., inpatient treatment for drug addiction or severe eating disorder) or continuous forms of treatment without interruption because of semester or summer breaks are appro-priate for off-campus referrals.

Aside from the specific types of problems they present, students may not be good candidates for on-campus counseling services because of other factors. For example, students who do not appear to be motivated for counseling or report that they have not benefited from previous counseling experiences represent poor candidates for counseling. Amada (1999) argued that students should be disqualified from utilizing coun-seling services if they have illegitimate reasons for being in counseling or behave in ways that are disrespectful or abusive toward any counsel-ing center staff members. Also, students who, for whatever reason, can-not consistently participate in counseling (e.g., because they frequently cancel appointments) are not likely to benefit from counseling. Thus, in some cases, students may be declined ongoing counseling but still be eligible for services on an as-needed basis whereas in other cases students may be excluded from using campus counseling services altogether.

Though most counseling centers may vary somewhat in terms of the criteria they use for referring into the community, they will need to refer at least some percentage of students to off-campus resources. A recent survey found that close to 10% of counseling center clients are referred out to external practitioners for more specialized or inten-sive treatment (Gallagher, 2010). Smaller counseling centers, how-ever, tend to arrange for fewer outside referrals than larger centers (Vespia, 2007).

Despite the obvious need to refer students to off-campus resources in certain cases, the process of doing so can be problematic. There are a variety of factors that can influence the referral process (Gage & Gyorky, 1990; Lawe, Penick, Raskin, & Raymond, 1999; Quintana, Yesenosky, Kilmartin, & Macias, 1991), with financial issues, such as limited finances and lack of insurance coverage, being a primary obstacle to successful referrals (Lacour & Carter, 2002; Owen, Devdas, & Rodolfa, 2007; Quintana et al., 1991). It can be quite challenging to find affordable practitioners for students in the surrounding community. Students who are on their parents' insurance plans may not necessarily want to involve their parents in their treatment, thereby eliminating that as an option. There can also be problems for students in terms of finding transportation or the time to commute to off-campus locations. In addition, not all outside services will have the proper expertise or be appropriate for college student mental health issues.

On the basis of a sample of counseling center clients who were referred out, Owen et al. (2007) found that 42% had not actually followed through with the referral. In addition to financial issues, another key factor that influenced the likelihood of a referral being successful was the student's perceived need and personal level of motivation for counseling. The more students experience a need and motivation for counseling, the more likely they will make a connection to an off-campus professional when referred. The researchers also found that outside referrals are more successful when college counselors follow up with the clients they refer out. Thus, although there are ways to enhance the success of making off-campus referrals, college counselors cannot necessarily rely on this as a strategy per se for easing the high demand for services.

Working Within the Administrative Structure

An interesting dimension of college counseling is the need to work within an administrative structure under the direction of administrators who may or may not have a clear understanding of college counseling. On most campuses, counseling services are administratively housed within the division of student affairs or student services, with the director of counseling reporting to the vice president, associate vice president, or assistant vice president of that division. At some institutions, the director will report to the dean of students or other administrator within student affairs who in turn reports to a higher level administrator. A smaller number of counseling centers are administratively housed within the division of academic affairs, with the director reporting to the vice president (or provost), associate vice president, or assistant vice president of that division.

Regardless of whom the director reports to, he or she needs to maintain a strong and positive relationship with that individual. Because it is not uncommon for there to be misperceptions or misunderstandings of what college counselors can and cannot do (Much, Wagener, & Hellenbrand, 2010), it is important that college counselors educate others (particularly the administrators they report to) about their services. It is particularly vital that the mission, goals, and policies of a counseling center be consistent with the mission, goals, and policies of the division within which it is administratively housed as well as the larger institution (Herr, Heitzmann, & Rayman, 2006). College counselors (especially directors) need to demonstrate their value and show how counseling services contribute to the overall mission of their universities. As an example, this might consist of showing connections between counseling and student retention (Sharkin, 2004b) or how college counselors provide valuable support for underrepresented student groups on campus. College counseling centers cannot operate in a vacuum but must establish themselves as a critical component of the functioning of the university.

Despite the best efforts of college counselors, a positive relationship with administrators who oversee their services is not guaranteed. Administrators can fall anywhere on a continuum from being highly supportive advocates on the most positive end to openly adversarial and hostile at the most negative end. It is possible to have a relationship with an administrator that sways along varying points on the continuum. At some institutions, the quality of working relationships with administrators may reflect a trickle-down effect from the highest level, namely, the president or chancellor. If counseling services are perceived as valuable by those at the highest level of administration, then there will usually be few problems encountered at the lower levels. Conversely, when counseling is not highly valued by those at the highest level, relationships are more likely to be strained between college counselors and the administrators they report to.

In addition to the quality of relationships between college counselors and administrators, it is also important for college counselors to have good working relationships with colleagues within their division and throughout the university. As has often been referenced in this book, there are a number of offices and individuals with whom college counselors need to collaborate, whether for consultations about students, committee work, or multidisciplinary treatment teams. Perhaps the "top 10" departments (not in rank order) in this regard would be (a) the Dean of Students office, (b) Health Services, (c) Public Safety or Campus Police, (d) Residential Life, (e) Disability Support Services, (f) Multicultural Services, (g) Career Services, (h) Academic Support Services, (i) Financial Aid, and (j) Department of Counseling (if such an academic program exists on campus, and if one's counseling center is involved in training activities). The forging of good relationships with these offices is important, though not necessarily critical, for college counselors to fulfill their duties.

It is inevitable that, for a variety of reasons, there may be some difficulties establishing positive relationships with some of these identified departments and others on campus. There is nothing more disconcerting and disheartening than to have strained relations with other individuals or departments on campus. Such strains can sometimes interfere with efforts to provide the best quality care and effective services to students. Thus, it is important that college counselors make every effort to maintain positive relationships with other departments and to take steps to repair damaged relationships. For example, college counselors can invite others to be guests during staff meetings or offer to be guests in their meetings to discuss topics of mutual interest. Sometimes strains result from the need for counselors to maintain confidentiality of their counseling work with students, as this can occasionally irk administrators and others on campus who say they understand the principle of confidentiality but still expect counselors to divulge confidential information. These and other challenges associated with the maintenance of boundaries will be addressed in the next section.

Maintaining Boundaries

College counselors often find themselves walking a fine line between their ethical obligation to protect client confidentiality and their need to work collaboratively with others on campus in addressing concerns regarding students. College counselors have to find ways to communicate with administrators, faculty, and others who may have a need to be informed about students but never at the expense of breaking client confidentiality. Of course, there are situations in which confidentiality is not a restriction on a counselor's freedom to communicate with others, for example, when a parent calls to convey concern about a student before any counseling relationship has been established with the student. It is a different matter when information is sought regarding a current or former client. College counselors must maintain confidentiality regarding their clients unless they have written client consent to release information.

The college campus is an environment that lends itself all too well to informal discussions among professional colleagues. College counselors are likely to have encounters with deans, professors, and others in informal campus settings such as in a cafeteria or on a sidewalk, and they may be asked questions about specific students during these encounters. The dilemmas and pressures for college counselors associated with such informal (and more formal) requests for confidential information from others has been well documented (Birky, Sharkin, Marin, & Scappaticci, 1998; Gilbert, 1989; Hayman & Covert, 1986; Malley, Gallagher, & Brown, 1992; Sharkin, 1995; Sharkin, Scappaticci, & Birky, 1995).

As any counselor or therapist can attest, confidentiality is the cornerstone of counseling. People will not engage in counseling unless they can trust that their disclosures will not be revealed without their knowledge and consent. However, to some third parties, confidentiality represents an annoying obstacle that can generate negative reactions (Birky et al., 1998; Sharkin, 1995). It is understandable when referral agents want to follow up on students they refer to counseling, but they need to understand and respect the ethical principle of confidentiality adhered to by counselors. Thus, it is incumbent on college counselors to educate others on campus about the confidential nature of counseling and the appropriate ways to arrange for client consent for shared information between counselors and others (Sharkin, 2006).

Another boundary issue that can pose unique challenges for college counselors is the issue of dual (or multiple) relationships that can result from the multiple roles of counselors on campus. Such dual-role situations are often unavoidable and can place strains on confidentiality (R. S. Harris, 2002; Iosupovici & Luke, 2002; Malley et al., 1992; Much et al., 2010; Sharkin, 1995). Dual-role relationships are especially likely to occur on small campuses (Grayson, 1986; Vespia, 2007). There are a variety of dual relationships in which college counselors can find themselves (R. S. Harris, 2002); for example, encountering a client while facilitating an outreach program or being on a committee that has a student representative who is a current or former client. College counselors often have chance or incidental encounters with clients in various locations on and off campus, which can be potentially awkward and pose strains on the maintenance of confidentiality (Sharkin, 1995). Because of these situations, college counselors are continually challenged to maintain proper boundaries without appearing overly rigid or unapproachable to students, faculty, and staff.

Anxiety About Lawsuits

Concerns and anxieties about malpractice lawsuits within the domain of college counseling have been addressed in years past (e.g., Slimak & Berkowitz, 1983), yet the perception of increasing liability from more recent highly publicized lawsuits appears to be making many college counselors uneasy about the prospect of litigation. Is this anxiety justified? The answer is yes and no. There is always an element of risk when practicing any type of mental health counseling. For college counselors, vulnerability to litigation can stem from issues of confidentiality, record keeping (and release of records), assessment and evaluation of students, suicide prevention, potential dangerousness or risk of harm to others posed by students, hospitalization of students, involuntary or mandated leaves, and dual relationships (Affsprung, 2010). Although practicing in an ethical and professional manner will undoubtedly lessen one's liability significantly, even the most ethical and conscientious practitioner can be vulnerable to legal action in certain cases.

On a reassuring note, however, the degree of litigation brought against college counselors appears to be relatively low. This suggests that anxieties about lawsuits may tend to be unfounded. In an examination of legal action taken against counseling centers over a 23-year period (1986–2008), Affsprung (2010) found that, on average, not more than 1% of centers were involved in any litigation. Of the total cases, many were either settled out of court or decided in favor of the counseling center. Although relatively rare, when legal action was taken by students or family members of students, it most frequently involved inappropriate behavior on the part of the counselor (e.g., knowingly entering into an inappropriate relationship with a client). The next most common form of malpractice had to do with cases in which a failure to prevent suicide was alleged. Thus, for college counselors to minimize their liability risk, they must be particularly vigilant to avoid any type of improper boundaries with clients and take all steps necessary to ensure the safety of students deemed at risk for suicide.

Another reason that was found to precipitate litigation in Affsprung's (2010) analysis of cases was wrongful hospitalization. Perhaps because of anxieties associated with not preventing student suicide, college counselors may sometimes err in the direction of trying to have students hospitalized when that is not necessarily warranted. In general, colleges seem to have responded to the increase in high-profile lawsuits by taking more drastic measures in the hope of lessening their liability. This has consisted of risk management strategies such as mandated assessment, mandated counseling, involuntary withdrawal, and evictions from on-campus housing. Rather than reduce liability risk, however, such tactics may actually increase the degree of risk, as more and more students have challenged these decisions (Pavela, 2006; R. B. Smith & Fleming, 2007). As noted previously, university policies and practices must avoid infringing on students' due process rights and violating the Americans With Disabilities Act. Because many of the risk management actions, such as involuntary withdrawal, may try to rely on the input or expertise of mental health professionals, it behooves college counselors to carefully consider the scope of their role in these decisions. It may be preferable for administrators to rely more on outside professionals in such cases in order to preserve the reputation of college counselors as administratively neutral and not directly linked to disciplinary or other administrative decisions (Boyd et al., 2003). This issue will be further examined in the next two subsections of this chapter.

Related to the issue of liability and risk management is the question of whether college counselors are sufficiently covered by their university's general liability coverage or should carry their own professional liability insurance. Based on informal discussions among counseling center professionals over the years, the feelings seem to be mixed on this issue. Some college counselors are comfortable with the notion that they are adequately covered as employees of their institutions, whereas others fear that their institutions cannot provide adequate coverage or representation in the event of a lawsuit. There may be concern that the institution's lawyer(s) will put the best interests of the institution before the best interests of the individual employee. For example, universities may prefer to settle a case rather than face litigation, which may not always be in the best interest of the individual employee. In addition, universities are not likely to provide legal representation when complaints are filed against individuals through their state licensing board. Although there are no data readily available to show how many college counselors have their own personal liability insurance, it can be assumed that those who concurrently maintain a private practice are likely to have such additional coverage.

The Increasing Role in Threat Assessment

As a result of the tragedy at Virginia Tech, colleges stepped up their efforts to prevent any future cases of violence or murder by instituting procedures for threat assessment on their campuses. It is understandable that the expertise of campus mental health professionals would be called on to help determine the potential danger posed by students. College counselors have long worked under legal and ethical mandates to warn and protect potential victims of harm identified by their clients. A recent survey of counseling centers (Gallagher, 2010) found that 20% of centers had at least one incident in which they needed to give a warning (to police, the potential victim, and/or others) about a student who posed a specific danger to someone. However, the increasing role of college counselors in campus-wide threat assessment efforts may have negative consequences in the long run. Some of the potential complications for college counselors related to their involvement in the threat assessment process can be illustrated simply by looking at what transpired at Virginia Tech well before Seung-Hui Cho committed mass murder.

Before the Shootings at Virginia Tech

In the aftermath of such a terrible event, it is normal for questions to subsequently emerge as to what could have been done to prevent it from happening. In the case of the shootings at Virginia Tech, scrutiny was eventually directed at the counseling center staff members who had knowledge about or contact with Cho and whether they should be held accountable for not doing enough to protect the campus community. Questions as to the role of counseling center staff in not preventing the shootings will be closely examined in legal proceedings. As noted in Chapter 1, lawsuits filed against Virginia Tech by the families of two students who were killed that day are still pending. Upon further scrutiny, certain issues may help exonerate the counselors in this case.

First and foremost, it is extremely difficult to make accurate predictions of violent behavior when an individual makes no overt threat or denies any thoughts of harming others, as was allegedly the case with Cho. There is no doubt that Cho behaved in ways that aroused concern, but there was no indication that he had the potential to commit murder, let alone mass murder. As with another campus shooting that occurred at Northern Illinois University (NIU) less than a year after the Virginia Tech tragedy, there were few clues that former NIU graduate student Steven Kazmierczak was going to open fire in a lecture hall, killing five people and then himself.

Second, there are indeed restrictions on communication between different offices on a campus, and in fact the Virginia Tech Review Panel (2007) made note of widespread confusion regarding what is and is not allowed to be shared under federal and state privacy laws.

Paterson and Colbs (2008) similarly highlighted the frequent mis-understanding and misinterpretation of student privacy laws, includ-ing the Family Educational Rights and Privacy Act (FERPA), the Health Insurance Portability and Accountability Act, and state laws governing mental health records. They maintain that several issues need to be considered when dealing with privacy laws, such as the determination of *who* needs to be informed about a student and *when* such a disclosure needs to occur. Paterson and Colbs pointed out that it can be tricky to balance the best interests of individuals against the best interests of a community when attempting to prevent harm. Flynn and Heitzmann (2008) raised similar concerns about trying to protect client confidentiality while at the same time having to ensure a safe campus. It is unclear at this point, but the counselors who had direct or indirect knowledge about Cho may have determined that communication with others on campus, with or without his consent, was unwarranted.

Whether any of the counselors should have made contact with Cho's parents also remains unclear. Although the Virginia Tech case prompted the U.S. Department of Education to amend FERPA regu-lations to allow universities more freedom to contact parents (without student consent), doing so is not always in the best interest of the student or university. Thus, any decisions regarding communication with Cho's parents would have needed to factor in the potential for them to be helpful versus to make matters worse. At times, contact with parents can be helpful, but in certain situations this can actually trigger more anxiety, anger, stress, and potentially heightened suicide risk for students. Also, it is unknown whether Cho would have agreed to allow a counselor to contact his parents. If contact had been made against his wishes, it would have damaged the prospect of establishing a therapeutic relationship with someone in the counseling center and could have contributed to increased risk of self-harm or harm to others. It would also have opened up liability for breaking confidentiality.

Third, if in fact Cho was court ordered to enter treatment at the counseling center (whether or not this was known by center counsel-ors), this could have posed ethical dilemmas or policy violations, as many counseling centers do not see involuntary referrals for counsel-ing regardless of the mandated referral source. It has been reported that Virginia Tech's counseling center has such a policy against doing involuntary treatment (Shuchman, 2007). Mandated counseling for college students is a controversial issue and considered by some college counselors to be ineffective, unethical, and potentially counter-therapeutic (Kiracofe & Buller, 2009; Sharkin, 2007). This issue will be further addressed later in this chapter.

The one matter that is indefensible in the Virginia Tech case is the discovery of Cho's records in the home of the former center director. For some unknown reason, the records had been removed more than a year before the shootings when Dr. Richard Miller left Virginia Tech. According to news reports, Cho's records (and those of a few other students) were "inadvertently" packed in with Dr. Miller's other belongings when he cleaned out his office in February 2006 (Schulte & Jackman, 2009). After Dr. Miller was named in the wrongful death lawsuit, he was ordered to do a search of his home, whereupon he discovered the records. Considering that Dr. Miller had no direct contact with Cho and that the records went missing *well before* the shootings, this appears to be a case of simple carelessness and not some sort of cover-up. However, it is improper for a clinician to remove such records from a counseling office, and even the appearance of impropriety in this case can be only problematic for the defendants in the lawsuit.

As this case demonstrates, it is not always such an easy matter of "connecting the dots" when dealing with troubled students. It is particularly challenging to determine if there is any potential for a student to act out in violent or harmful ways, especially when no specific threats of violence against others are made by the student. To fairly assess the actions taken by the counselors, one must try to imagine what could have been done under the circumstances and not having any indication whatsoever that Cho would commit mass murder on the campus nearly a year and a half later. This is a huge time lag between when Cho was seen in the counseling center and when he committed mass murder.

The Jared Lee Loughner Case

The more recent case of Jared Lee Loughner represents another and perhaps better example of the limitations of what an institution can realistically do when no specific or direct threats are involved. Loughner killed 6 people and wounded 14 others (including U.S. Representative Gabrielle Giffords) in Tucson, Arizona, on January 8, 2011. Although the shootings did not occur on a college campus, subsequent reports quickly surfaced about Loughner's troubling behavior some months prior while he was a student at Pima Community College (PCC) in Tucson. We learned, for example, that Loughner was involved in several incidents, including disruptive behavior in class such as bizarre outbursts, which prompted calls to campus police (Sulzberger & Gabriel, 2011). As a result, he was suspended from the school in September 2010, with his reinstatement contingent on his obtaining a letter from a mental health professional to attest that he posed no danger to himself or others. According to reports, the school did not make any attempt to have him undergo a mandatory mental health evaluation (Sulzberger & Gabriel, 2011), which would have had to be off campus because PCC does not have any mental health professionals on campus. Most recently, a federal judge ruled that Loughner is not mentally competent to stand trial in the shootings.

If there had been a threat assessment team in place at PCC, this student most likely would have come to its attention, perhaps as early as the first incident of inappropriate or odd behavior. Because this particular school did not have any mental health resources on campus, its options were limited. It is possible that Loughner would have been referred for an evaluation by a mental health professional on campus if that had been available. Once the tragic shootings occurred, as in the Virginia Tech and other such cases, questions began to emerge as to what could or should have been done so that the eventual tragedy might have been averted. The way PCC handled the problems with Loughner came under scrutiny and criticism, particularly the fact that the college did not arrange for him to be evaluated. Certainly the college could have done that by applying for a court-ordered mental health evaluation. However, that may not have been considered necessary if Loughner did not make any overt threats to harm anyone (e.g., did he pose a risk of harm that was reasonably foreseeable?). It appears that the college primarily responded to his troubling behavior from a disciplinary perspective, though it was clear that he needed to seek a mental health evaluation before he could be reinstated.

Once again, this case demonstrates that it is not always clear-cut as to how a student who displays some form of mental disturbance should be handled by the institution. Although there was evidence to suggest that Loughner was experiencing delusional ideation and increasing paranoia, this does not necessarily mean that he should be considered dangerous or that he was subsequently going to be dangerous to others. Colleges need to be careful not to overreact and violate student rights when it is not justified to do so.

Concerns About the Broadening Role of College
Counselors and "Mental Health Profiling"

The increasing role of college counselors in threat assessment has raised some serious concerns. For example, Davenport (2009) wondered about the possible negative consequences that may accrue from the ever-increasing, broadened role of college counselors in the domain of campus safety. Administrators and others are likely to rely more and more on college counselors for assessments of students' propensity to act violently, even though the prediction of violent behavior is far from an exact science. Davenport said that this role for college counselors, if it becomes more prominent, could compromise the quality of their care with students by fostering the perception of college counselors as an extension of campus safety. Despite these concerns, it is inevitable that others on campus, for better or worse, will continue to turn to college counselors for their perceived expertise in assessing risk of student dangerousness and violence.

Another concern related to the process of threat assessment is the potential harm that may result from this new form of "campus surveillance" and "mental health profiling" of students who display eccentric or odd behavior but not necessarily threatening behavior (Reiss, 2011). This type of profiling is analogous to the ethnic profiling that occurred following the September 11th terrorist attacks. Given that all of the terrorists were males from countries in the Middle East, a profile emerged based on this demographic. In a similar manner, a profile of "psychologically disturbed" males may now represent the profile of the "dangerous" college student, even though these students may not pose any danger more so than any other student. In other words, the myth of mental illness being equated with the propensity for violence will become reinforced in people's minds.

Reiss further observed that the increased reliance on behavioral intervention and threat assessment teams has not yet been proven to ensure safety on campuses. To date, there has been no evidence put forth that the actions of these teams make campuses safer, and they may actually make campuses overly vigilant to signs of potential violence. Nevertheless, campuses have been moving forward with such protocols at a rapid pace. Perhaps colleges view the benefits of having threat assessment protocols in place as outweighing any potential harm or risks that may result from them.

As already discussed, a key component of conducting threat assessment is to have students evaluated, oftentimes against their will. Depending on the outcome of such an evaluation, some students may be further mandated to participate in counseling. This, of course, has a direct impact on college counselors, for they are often the ones being asked to perform the mandated evaluation and provide the mandated counseling. The ongoing debate over this issue will be discussed in the following section.

Increasing Pressure to Conduct Mandated Assessments and Mandated Counseling

As indicated in the previous section, college counselors are experiencing increasing pressure to conduct mandated assessments and mandated counseling. Mandated referrals are often made under the presumption that problematic behavior involves some type of underlying emotional issue, such as poor impulse control or poor anger management. The practice of mandating students to undergo an evaluation or participate in counseling is likely to grow in conjunction with the growing numbers of behavioral intervention and threat assessment teams on campuses.

There is clearly no consensus among college counselors on the issue of mandated interventions with students. In one survey of counseling center directors (Gallagher, 2009), centers were found to differ widely in their position on mandated referrals: 34% reported that they would accept mandated referrals for both assessments and counseling, 57% agreed to do mandated assessments but not mandated counseling, and 9% reported that they would not accept any mandated referrals. The position of the Association of University and College Counseling Center Directors on the subject may best represent the majority perspective: There can be value in performing mandated assessments in cases of clear problematic behavior and violation of conduct codes. However, the organization is opposed to mandated counseling on the grounds that it is a violation of the ethical principle of *autonomy* for clients of counseling. As previously noted, the International Association of Counseling Services also allows for mandated assessments as long as counseling centers avoid direct involvement in disciplinary actions and decisions.

In many respects, agreeing to do mandated assessments or evaluations without having any apparent role in disciplinary decisions is an inherently flawed proposition. When students are required to see a campus counselor as a result of some type of disciplinary matter or violation of student conduct, the counselor is in fact part of the disciplinary process, no matter how one looks at it. Counselors need to report back to the referral source, oftentimes the dean of students, with their concerns or impressions. Although college counselors can argue that they are serving only as consultants to administrators and have no role in administrative or disciplinary decisions, the fact is that students will view their mandated session with a counselor as part of their disciplinary sanctions or "punishment." As Gilbert (1989) and Francis (2000) both observed, college counselors need to be wary of inadvertently serving as an unofficial enforcer for the school's administration, which can pose serious concerns about the integrity and perception of counseling centers as an impartial entity on campus. Such sentiment suggests that college counselors should generally avoid doing any mandated interventions if they involve disciplinary matters. In cases of concern about student suicide risk, most college counselors would agree that an assessment, even if involuntary, is warranted. Such cases, however, typically do not involve disciplinary-related decisions.

The primary reason that many college counselors will agree to do mandated assessments and/or mandated counseling is that they feel they have a responsibility to the institution that supports their services and must find ways to work together with administrators and others in dealing with problematic students (Francis, 2000). Ideally, off-campus mental health professionals would be used for mandated interventions, but this is not always feasible or practical. Who else can intervene in such cases? Perhaps it is preferable to have students who are disciplined participate in "educational" programs (e.g., about responsibly using alcohol or making responsible choices and decisions) conducted by staff members other than college counselors. This alternative approach would preserve the integrity of college counseling and protect already limited counseling resources from being misused.

Risks Associated With New Technology

As with most health professionals in today's world, college counselors have to grapple with a variety of concerns related to the increasing reliance on electronic technology to communicate with students, schedule students, document contacts with students, and store sensitive data about students. This includes online or electronic communication such as e-mail and computer software programs for scheduling and data storage. New technology is helping to improve the practice of counseling (Tyler & Sabella, 2004) while at the same time creating new risks to manage (Baron, Bierschwale, & Bleiberg, 2006; R. W. Mitchell, 2007; Richards, 2009).

Electronically Transmitted Communication

Even if college counselors do not use online counseling per se, they often communicate with students using electronic mail (Baron et al., 2006). Communications can range from simple matters such as rescheduling appointments to providing more involved responses to students' personal disclosures. College counselors may also use e-mail to correspond with others on campus regarding concerns about students or for follow-up on students referred for counseling. As an example, a college counselor may need to contact a student's professor(s) when a student's emotional difficulties result in missed classes, exams, or assignments.

The use of electronically transmitted communications can be risky because of the difficulties with maintaining confidentiality (R. W. Mitchell, 2007). There are a number of scenarios in which unauthorized individuals can gain access to confidential information. Others who share a computer with a student (e.g., family members or roommates) can easily see what is on the student's computer and may be able to view e-mail messages, especially if the student remains online and then leaves the computer unattended. If an e-mail address is mistyped, the information may be sent to someone else (unless the address does not exist). Given that some students have similar or identical names, counselors may inadvertently send messages to the wrong person. The use of a student's name in an e-mail (identifying the student as a client) might be read by or forwarded to someone who has no need to have that information.

There are some suggested ways to at least minimize negative consequences of such potential mishaps. It has been suggested that only initials or first names be used rather than full names in e-mail (R. W. Mitchell, 2007). Many college counselors will now include disclaimers about the limited security of confidentiality in e-mail correspondence with or about students who are clients and request that messages be deleted if sent to the wrong person. Some e-mail systems now allow the sender to mark messages as "confidential." Counselors can also check with students at the beginning of counseling to see how they prefer to contact or be contacted by the counselor, specifically whether they would prefer to use e-mail correspondence or avoid it altogether. For students who want the option of using e-mail, counselors can then inform them of the limitations and potential abuses of that form of communication.

Student Cell Phone Use

Mobile or cell phone use is so common among today's college students that this seems to be the primary mode (other than e-mail) of contacting students. When it becomes necessary for college counselors or counseling center support staff to call students, cell phones are actually preferable to residential landline phones because they tend to be private and not shared with others. This is especially true when voicemail messages need to be left for a student. With residential phones, for instance, a message can be left but only if the voicemail is specifically for that student and not a shared voicemail (or answering machine). This is generally the case even if students give permission for messages from the counseling center to be left on a shared line. Another positive aspect of cell phones is that they can come in handy whenever there may be a need to contact parents (e.g., during a crisis situation). If a student is amenable to contact with parents, he or she can be the one to initially call them using his or her cell phone so that parents know whom the call is from.

Despite the obvious advantages of cell phones, there are some issues related to cell phone use to which college counselors need to remain sensitive. First, when students receive calls on their cell phones, they can be just about anywhere and with anybody. It is often necessary to first check with the student to see if it is an appropriate time to speak with him or her, even if simply to reschedule an appointment. Second, cell phones are not always reliable, and calls can be difficult to hear or suddenly lost. This is especially challenging for college counselors who need to speak to students during emergency or crisis calls. Third, as most professors will attest, student cell phones are often kept on during class and other events. Counseling sessions are no exception. It is not that uncommon to have a student's cell phone ring during a counseling session. For college counselors, this can be considered anything from a minor nuisance to a more serious distraction. As such, some counselors may ask students, as a general rule, to turn their phones off during sessions, similar to professors asking students to silence their phones during class.

Another interesting aspect of cell phone use that should be mentioned is the now commonplace use of text messaging. As has been the case with e-mail, students will often send text messages to family members or friends (who may be students on the campus) conveying their distress. In some instances, the message may contain references to suicide or be interpreted as suicidal in nature. Thus, text messages of this sort now represent an increasingly common scenario in which college counselors will be asked to intervene. For example, a student who receives a suicidal message from another student may first contact the counseling center or will contact someone who will then contact the counseling center. In such instances, it is helpful for the counselor to see the actual message to assist in determining the seriousness of the threat.

Websites and Internet Social Networking

Most, if not all, counseling centers will have a website, typically as a link within student services. These websites are sometimes the way that students first make contact with the counseling center. One of the major advantages of a website is that it is a quick and convenient way to inform students, faculty, and staff about the counseling center. The website can provide links to other sites and resources for important information related to college student mental health. A website will also usually allow for direct contact with the center using the e-mail address of a designated contact person or a generic e-mail address that may go to a support staff member. These e-mails may be simple queries about the center, such as how to schedule an appointment. Contacts initiated this way can also be somewhat more complicated. For example, a student may send an e-mail message through the site that conveys some sense of urgency to see a counselor.

Given the possibility of this latter type of situation, it is advised that counseling center websites include a disclaimer that would inform users that matters of urgency should not be directed to the center through e-mail. Centers can set up a system for checking and responding to e-mail messages sent through the website, but students and others need to understand that there can sometimes be delays in the timeliness of a response. Website visitors can be encouraged to call the counseling center during regular hours and informed about whom to call for emergencies or situations that occur after hours (e.g., counseling center on call, local crisis intervention service, public safety, etc.).

Another issue related to center websites is who is responsible for maintaining the site and making sure that links are accurate and up-to-date. A specific staff member may need to be designated to be the office website manager. Some centers may find creative ways to use their websites. As an example, Doumas and Anderson (2009) devised a web-based feedback program designed to reduce heavy alcohol consumption among first-year students. Websites certainly have the potential to enable college counselors to reach out to students in ways that were previously not possible.

In addition to their own websites, counseling centers are increasingly using social network or media websites like Facebook as a way to have an online presence. Given that today's college students are so heavily involved with such websites, college counselors are recognizing the value of using this technology to engage students in a new and different way. This may include the creation of blogs, in which college counselors post material relevant for students (e.g., dating and relationship issues) and then allow students to post their comments and reactions. Some counseling centers are creating Facebook pages as an alternative to the traditional website in order to connect with students. Some college counselors may begin to explore the feasibility of online counseling, at least in certain situations in which traditional face-to-face counseling is not possible (e.g., a student studying abroad). Although these new uses of social networks and online counseling present new and previously unimagined possibilities for college counselors, they also pose new ethical challenges (Parish & Friedman, 2011). For example, counselors must be especially vigilant about maintaining proper boundaries with students, given that social networking websites such as Facebook may allow for more mutual personal disclosure and blurring of professional boundaries (Parish & Friedman, 2011).

One final issue that deserves mention here is what appear to be secondhand effects of electronic and cyber-based forms of communication that are now commonplace in the lives of students. It is not unusual to have students present in distress because of problems associated with text messages, instant messages, e-mail, social networks, and the like. For example, a student may become upset by something that is written about him or her or because of being defriended or blocked from a friend's Facebook page. Students may be susceptible to spending inordinate amounts of time on such sites and the Internet, sometimes to the point of it being an addiction. Some students may actually post thoughts or experiences on a social network site that arouses concern from others. Whether these new forms of cyber communication are positive or negative is debatable, but there is no question that they are now firmly entrenched in the everyday lives of today's college students.

Electronic Records

The use of electronic records offers a number of advantages over using written records. Electronic records eliminate the problems of dealing with poor or illegible handwriting. The use of electronic or computer software programs for scheduling and data storage helps in the effort to go paperless and be ecologically friendly. Another advantage is the quick and easy access that it affords compared with searching for and through papers kept in files. Although old-fashioned files may not yet be totally obsolete, for some minimal information can still be kept in files, they will certainly be reduced in size and how much storage space they require.

As more and more counseling centers convert to electronic records, a number of unique issues and challenges continue to emerge. With electronic records, there can never be 100% protection (R. W. Mitchell, 2007; Richards, 2009). The potential for abuse can come from a variety of sources. Perhaps the biggest concern is with improper access by unauthorized users (R. W. Mitchell, 2007). With so much sensitive information that is entered into college counseling records, such as dates of service, case notes, diagnostic information, and information about medications, there needs to be clear guidelines and protocols for who can view data, enter new data, and/or edit existing data. Many records may also include other noncounseling-related sensitive information, such as social security and cell phone numbers, making the issue of protection from unauthorized access of paramount importance. In addition to password protection, other safeguards may be needed. For example, each user may need to enter a code to log on so that each user can be identified. Also, there should be a way to be able to verify log-ons and the date and time of all user activity.

Other problems that can occur with an electronic database system are the possibility of the system freezing or going down and invasion of a computer virus that alters or deletes data (Richards, 2009). Such problems could cause chaos and panic in a counseling center that relies on the system for viewing the daily schedule and storing student data. Thus, it is recommended that any system be backed up on a regular basis (e.g., using disks). As with website maintenance, someone in the counseling center may need to assume primary responsibility for overseeing the electronic record-keeping system. This is likely to be the center's director in most cases, though it could be delegated to a staff person with special expertise with computer systems. Aside from who has this primary duty, it is essential that all users receive proper training and supervision of electronic record keeping (R. W. Mitchell, 2007).

Special Challenges for Community College Counselors

Community colleges have long played a significant role in higher education. They often represent the first stepping-stone toward earning a bachelor's degree for many students, as well as provide students with valuable short-term training and job skills. With the current economic recession, increasing numbers of students are now viewing enrollment at a community college (before subsequently transferring to a 4-year institution) as a wise financial investment and an ideal way to prepare for the demands of a college career.

College counselors who work in a community college setting face some unique challenges above and beyond what most college counselors face. This is due to the fact that community colleges are generally designed to meet the needs of an extremely diverse student body and therefore need to offer a broad array of services (Dean, 2000). There can be a wide range of academic skills and abilities among community college students, with considerable diversity in terms of preparation for college. Indeed, some students may first need to take remedial courses because of deficiencies in preparation for college-level work. For example, community colleges often have many returning students who have been out of school for a number of years and need help relearning specific academic skills. Also, community college students often have limited access to health care and no health insurance, making it difficult to refer students to off-campus mental health professionals (C. Baker, personal communication, March 29, 2011).

Although community colleges vary in terms of the scope of counseling services they provide, there are some characteristics that many appear to have in common. Data about community college counselors have been obtained from a recent national (albeit small) LISTSERV survey of 67 community college counselors from over 50 different institutions by the American College Counseling Association's Community College Task Force (ACCA, 2009–2010). From the survey, it was found that the majority of community college counselors hold master's degrees (82%) and licensure as licensed mental health counselors or licensed professional counselors (55%). The average weekly client caseload for personal counseling can vary from 1 to 5 (23%), 6 to 10 (29%), 11 to 15 (20%), 16 to 20 (17%), and 21 to 30 (10%). Community college counseling services can be administratively housed within different divisions within the institution, though the survey found that a slight majority is based in student affairs or student development (51.5%).

One of the key features of being a community college counselor is the need to wear many hats, or as Dean (2000) once referred to it, the "one-stop shopping" model. This means that the emphasis is on offering multiple services, including personal counseling, career testing, academic advising, admissions and transfer advising, academic support services, support services for students in academic jeopardy and on probation, psychoeducational programming, continuing education, and disability services. There are also administrative duties and, in some instances, teaching responsibilities. As discussed throughout this book, college counselors at all institutions make contributions in many different domains in addition to personal counseling, including services provided by others on campus. However, the community college counselor may be *expected* to provide services in several other domains that are not offered elsewhere on the campus. Consider, for example, disability services. As discussed in Chapter 3, many 4-year institutions now have a disability services office or specialist, allowing college counselors to provide services in conjunction with these specialty services. Community college counselors, on the other hand, may be the only resource to provide disability services on campus, which will be *in addition to* personal counseling and other services. Also in contrast with college counselors at 4-year institutions, community college counselors are likely to be more directly involved in activities such as recruitment and orientation.

Given the many roles of community college counselors, they may find themselves working with some students in several different capacities. This can be quite positive in that they are in a good position to assist students with multiple issues and needs. It can also pose complications in terms of managing the multiple roles and maintaining proper boundaries with some students (Dean, 2000). For example, it would not be uncommon to work with students on emotional concerns such as anxiety while at the same time assisting with academic difficulties that may stem from or cause struggles with anxiety. In such cases, the counselor needs to decide how best to intervene; should the primary focus be on the emotional concerns, the academic concerns, or on both problems equally? Also, this poses ethical challenges for community college counselors. For example, if a licensed professional counselor provides counseling but also provides academic counseling, the counselor must make sure that there are clear boundaries such as distinguishing the counseling relationship by providing informed consent.

Another example involving potential boundary concerns would be when the counselor has worked with a student in one capacity and is then subsequently asked (or expected) to assume a different (and perhaps conflicting) role with the student. For example, imagine a counselor working with a student primarily on emotional concerns and then being asked to shift more attention to assisting the student with accommodations for a disability. The community college counselor may not have the option of referring the student for other services as a way to manage boundaries. The counselor must still let the student know that there is a shift into more personal counseling and clearly define this with informed consent.

Another significant difference between college counselors in community college settings and those in 4-year institutions is the fact that most community colleges are nonresidential settings. With most (if not all) students being commuters, it can be more challenging to intervene with troubled students. The residential component of 4-year colleges allows for more opportunities for others on campus, particularly residential life staff members, to check in or follow up with students who arouse concern. When concerns are expressed about students on a community college campus, especially in cases of perceived urgency, contact may need to be made with them when they are not on the campus. Such contact could inadvertently result in family members or others whom students live with being alerted to the fact that there are concerns. Although community college counselors may be likely to keep some evening hours, the vast majority does not provide after-hours emergency services (ACCA, 2009–2010). This can further hamper efforts to intervene with students if contact cannot be made during working hours and also makes it important to define the scope of practice in the counseling center.

Summary

College counselors face a number of challenges. One of the biggest challenges has been the struggle to continue to meet the ever-growing demand for counseling services as resources remain stagnant or dwindle. There are also challenges related to working within an administrative structure that may be unsupportive and perhaps even adversarial, working collaboratively within the campus community while also maintaining confidentiality of counseling and avoiding multiple relationships, managing anxieties about potential litigation, and handling increasing roles in threat assessment and mandated interventions for students. Like other professionals, college counselors are grappling with issues associated with new technologies, such as electronic forms of communication and electronic record keeping. In addition to these challenges faced by most college counselors on today's campus, community college counselors have to deal with some unique challenges related to aspects of the community college setting that can differ from those in the 4-year campus setting.

7

THE FUTURE OUTLOOK

Yogi Berra, known for his unintentionally funny quotes, once remarked, "The future ain't what it used to be." There is actually a lot of wisdom in that quote, especially as it pertains to the future of college counseling. The future outlook for the profession appeared much brighter several years ago. Of course, there have always been concerns about what the future had in store for the profession, for example, when concerns were first raised about the increasing severity of client problems (Bishop, 1990; Stone & Archer, 1990). But the overall health and potential growth of the profession tended to be strong despite being faced with a variety of challenges. The future of college counseling now seems much cloudier. With our faltering economy and pressures on colleges to contain costs, can colleges afford to continue to provide campus-based mental health services?

To try to answer this question, four key issues that are likely to receive increasing attention from college counselors and administrators in the coming years will be addressed: (a) the ever-looming threat of counseling services being outsourced on campuses as a cost-saving measure, (b) whether fees should be charged for counseling services, (c) whether colleges should fund or provide psychiatric services (primarily in the form of pharmacological treatment) on their campuses, and (d) consideration of merging counseling services with health services as a way to enhance resources. How each of these issues is likely to evolve in the coming years ahead will also be addressed.

Looming Threat of Outsourcing

Since the economic downturn began a few years ago, the mantra "doing more with less" has gradually been replaced with the mantra "doing less with less." Budgetary concerns are certainly not new in the world of college counseling. However, recent economic woes have perhaps created one of the most precarious periods for counseling as well as other types of student services. During such tough economic times, every campus program and activity comes under scrutiny. Because most counseling centers are funded either through their university's education and general budget or through mandatory student fees (e.g., student health fees) above and beyond tuition (Gallagher, 2010; Herr, Heitzmann, & Rayman, 2006), counseling services are at risk of being downsized, eliminated, or outsourced.

In today's climate in which risk management is essential, most institutions are unlikely to take drastic steps such as downsizing the scope of services or eliminating counseling services altogether if it increases the school's liability. Thus, outsourcing becomes appealing because it involves contracting with off-campus mental health agencies to provide services for a reduced cost. Colleges may be able to find local or regional agencies with whom they can contract to provide all necessary mental health services for students, including counseling, consultation with faculty and staff, and round-the-clock crisis intervention. Of course, the challenge is to contract for such services at a significantly lower cost than that of the traditional counseling center structure.

Even when significant cost reductions can be realized, however, the contract-for-service model is not without risks. Reverting to outsourcing may actually compromise services and the quality of care because it relies on outsiders rather than professionals who are part of the campus system (Bishop, 1995; Phillips, Halstead, & Carpenter, 1996; Widseth, Webb, & John, 1997). Outsourcing can compromise services in a number of ways. First and foremost, there would be a loss of expertise and understanding of college student mental health issues that traditional college counselors possess; outside professionals often have a more limited understanding of college student development and the academic environment or campus culture. Second, student access to and ease of entry into counseling may become more difficult. This would also be true for access to counselors for consultation by others on campus. Third, because outside providers are not really part of the campus system, they are not going to be perceived as true colleagues by campus faculty and staff, which could make the process of making referrals not only more difficult but less personal as well. Fourth, crisis intervention services are likely to be more limited because outside providers will typically not be as readily available or accessible as traditional college counselors. Fifth, there would be a loss of personnel to serve other functions on campus such as committee work, teaching, and research.

Indeed, there have been few instances where outsourcing has proven to be a truly viable option (Phillips et al., 1996). In cases where colleges did resort to outsourcing, many eventually reverted back to the traditional counseling center model to better serve the campus community (Phillips et al., 1996). Moreover, outsourcing may not necessarily be cost-effective; for example, there can be additional costs for an institution to monitor outsourced services and ensure that they are in compliance with the contract. Thus, a careful and thorough cost-benefit analysis would need to be conducted before an institution pursues the outsourcing of counseling services. Not all instances of outsourcing would be inappropriate. For example, it may make sense for some schools to contract with outside providers for emergency after-hours coverage. The bottom line is that whenever a university explores outsourcing, serious consideration needs to be given to the potential impact it would have on students.

Although many campuses are facing the prospect of budgetary cuts that could impact counseling services, there are some campuses where counseling services have actually expanded. Examples include NYU, MIT, and Virginia Tech. All of these schools had increases in their mental health budgets as a result of tragic events or litigation that received national attention. Consider the case of what happened at NYU. A string of suicides on that campus several years ago led to an overhaul and expansion of mental-health-related services (Winerip, 2011). The university increased the number of clinicians from 25 to 40, added a 24-hour hotline (which appears on the back of student ID cards), extended walk-in clinic hours for students in crisis, increased the number of on-campus psychiatrists, and instituted a training course for campus employees (such as those in the bursar's office and financial aid) to help them identify troubled students and how to diffuse difficult situations with students. Such cases of expansion of mental health services are perhaps the exception at the present time, and unfortunately needed some sort of tragedy to be instituted, but are a sign that some campuses are viewing mental health services as essential for their students.

For the campuses that simply do not have the resources to increase counseling resources, an alternative way to deal with budgetary short-falls would be to find ways to generate revenue. There may be several creative ways to supplement funding for counseling services. For example, counseling centers could explore options for offering continuing education programs, perhaps cosponsoring such programs with other departments on campus or off-campus agencies. College counselors could also apply for grants that might support specific components of their services (e.g., suicide prevention programming). The implementation of a fee-for-service component for counseling services is often explored (and in some cases adopted) as a way to offset the costs of staffing and maintaining a counseling center. The viability of charging fees will be explored in the next section.

Should Fees Be Charged for Counseling?

Before discussing the question of whether students should be charged fees for counseling, it is important to bear in mind that some counseling center budgets are supported, at least in part, by mandatory student fees, such as a health services fee (Gallagher, 2010; Herr et al., 2006). Any discussion of a fee-for-service model needs to consider that students, whether they utilize counseling or not, may already be paying fees that support counseling services on campus. Therefore, fees charged for counseling sessions may be in addition to these base fees already incurred by students.

The concept of charging fees for counseling has actually already been put into action on some campuses. National surveys of counseling center practices found that a small but significant percentage of centers charge fees: close to 7% in one survey (Gallagher, 2010) and 14% in another survey (Barr, Rando, Krylowicz, & Winfield, 2010). When fees are charged, they tend to be modest: The mean fee is $14, and the mean annual revenue from fees is about $41,000 (Gallagher, 2010).

There are different ways that fees can be assessed. Students can be charged for all of their appointments, appointments beyond a specified limit of free sessions, missed appointments, cancelled appointments with less than 24-hours notice, and specialized services, such as mandated alcohol assessments or psychological assessments. Most centers that charge fees do not do so for all appointments but typically do so under one or more of the other aforementioned conditions. Collecting third-party payments is another option, though a vast majority of centers do not do so (Barr et al., 2010; Gallagher, 2010).

The fee-for-service approach not only represents a way to generate revenue to help support counseling services but may also be effective in making the services more efficient, for example, by reducing missed appointments and preventing students from overutilizing counseling. On the flip side, however, the collection of fees requires additional time and resources to manage. This could further burden counseling centers already struggling to function with limited resources. Other complications include how to determine fees and whether any exceptions would apply. For instance, if students are charged for missed or cancelled appointments (with less than 24-hours notice), are there situations that would excuse students from being charged, and if so, who makes this determination? Would students be eligible to continue with counseling if they have an outstanding balance? Charging fees can raise ethical dilemmas as well; for example, how to maintain confidentiality when unpaid fees need to be applied to student accounts through the bursar's office. Another ethical dilemma would be how to handle students who often present in crisis but do not pay fees consistently. Would certain exceptions need to be made in which fees are waived? What about students who have limited financial resources? Would a sliding scale need to be implemented, and if so, how would it be determined? It could become problematic if students discover that fees are variable or are charged in some instances but not in others.

Hence, although the idea of imposing fees does have some appeal, it could pose a number of additional challenges to counseling centers already barely able to keep their heads above water. Unfortunately, however, this may be an inevitable course for the future of college counseling. Like so many other services provided by colleges and universities, be it meal plans, housing, and flu vaccinations, there is usually an added cost that students need to incur. The days of providing free counseling (or counseling based on a relatively small annual student fee) may eventually come to an end. This is certainly a better option than outsourcing, for despite having to resolve a number of issues when instituting a fee-for-service model, it would at least preserve the integrity and tradition of providing college counseling within the fabric of the campus setting.

Should Campuses Provide Psychiatric Services?

Psychiatric services are currently provided on many campuses. Based on recent surveys (Barr et al., 2010; Gallagher, 2010), over 50% of counseling centers provide or have access to on-campus psychiatric services. These services are often based within the counseling center or are provided at another site on campus, such as in health services. Although the practice of prescribing psychotropic medication is the primary domain of psychiatrists, other medical professionals such as general practice physicians and nurse practitioners can and do prescribe these kinds of medications. Psychiatric services may be especially critical on campuses where such medical professionals are reluctant to prescribe psychotropic medications or otherwise place restrictions on when and what type of psychotropic medications they will prescribe.

Based on recent surveys, the average number of hours per week for on-campus psychiatric services is 20 to 25 (Barr et al., 2010; Gallagher, 2010). According to Gallagher's (2010) survey, 14% of clients were referred for psychiatric evaluations, and 24% of clients were currently on psychotropic medication. These numbers suggest that a sizable proportion of students who seek services in their counseling center are using or will use psychotropic medication for their symptoms.

Clearly, then, there appears to be a need for psychiatric services on campus. In fact, in their survey, Barr et al. (2010) found that 50% of counseling centers indicated that they could use more hours of psychiatric services based on campus need. The numbers of students using medication are likely to continue to increase over the coming years. The movement toward brief treatment models in college counseling (especially given the high demand for services) has contributed to a greater reliance on medications. Medications are now readily available and can be effective in helping students cope with symptoms of depression, bipolar disorder, acute anxiety, panic attacks, social anxiety, and other mental health disorders. Use of medication may be particularly helpful in cases in which students are not able to function well enough to keep pace with their academic work. Although some students need to leave school periodically because of symptoms that interfere with academic demands, many more are able to remain in school because of the relatively fast relief from symptoms they can achieve by virtue of taking medication.

The use of medication to treat college students (and young people in general) does have a negative side that cannot be ignored. Concerns have been raised about the overmedicating of students and overreliance on medication to help students cope with everyday problems (Carter & Winseman, 2003). We now live in a culture in which we look for quick results for our problems, and for better or worse, there is a perception of medication as an effective quick fix. Many students may be more inclined to take a pill each day to alleviate symptoms causing distress rather than engage in counseling for several weeks with unknown results. But college counselors tend not to see medication as a panacea for student problems and prefer to see students use counseling in conjunction with medication. Another potential problem associated with prescribing psychotropic medication to students is that in many cases students may not be able to have follow-up medication checks when the school is not in session.

Although college counselors recognize the benefits of medication, they also know that medication use can have its own set of troubling consequences for students. Medications can have unpleasant side effects that may interfere with academic and social functioning. Students may be susceptible to misuse, dependency, or various forms of alcohol or drug abuse while on medication (Whitaker, 1992). Some students have been known to give or sell some of their prescribed medication to their peers, which can result in increased medical risk for those students using medication without proper supervision. It is for these reasons that some college counselors will refer students for medication only when there is a profound disruption in their day-to-day functioning.

Despite the limitations and potential complications of medication use among college students, it does appear that this growing trend of students on psychotropic medication is likely to continue into the future. Providing psychotropic medication to students on campus does give universities an additional form of liability to assume, and therefore many schools prefer to have students referred off campus for psychiatric services. However, a vast number of students simply do not have the resources or capability to seek such outside services. Furthermore, it can be preferable to have the option of arranging for a psychiatric evaluation on campus in cases involving students with debilitating forms of anxiety, clinical depression, or psychotic symptoms, because many students may not otherwise follow through with referrals off campus (Owen, Devdas, & Rodolfa, 2007).

Should Counseling Services Merge With Health Services?

An issue that has been receiving increasing attention from administrators is the question of whether counseling and health services should be integrated on campus (American College Health Association [ACHA], 2010). On most campuses, these two services are administratively housed within the same division (i.e., student services) and tend to work closely together. The relationship between the two services is important because of their shared concern for and treatment of students with problems such as anxiety, depression, eating disorders, sexual assault, and substance abuse. Students often first present in the health center with physical symptoms that are manifestations of emotional or psychological distress. On some campuses, psychiatric services are provided in the health center by physicians and nurse practitioners. Hence, there is clearly need for collaboration and in some cases a multidisciplinary approach to treatment.

In 2006, the ACHA created a Mental Health Best Practices Task Force, which collected and examined survey data regarding the merging of counseling and health services on college campuses. Although such mergers have been occurring for more than two decades, most counseling centers are not integrated with health services. According to the data collected by the ACHA Task Force, approximately 15% of counseling centers are fully integrated with health services, and another 15% share the same facility or building while remaining administratively independent.

As observed by the ACHA Task Force (2010), there can be advantages and disadvantages to merging counseling with health services. On the positive side, this represents a way to provide holistic care, improve the continuity of care, streamline resources, and place more emphasis on *wellness* services. On the negative side, mergers that may involve the sharing of records can compromise the confidentiality for students who seek services of both types. In addition, the differing philosophy of treatment of counseling versus that of health services may contribute to conflicts and disagreements, which in turn can result in the quality of care being compromised. In particular, the medical model ascribed to by many if not most campus health services is not always conducive to mental health treatment and in some instances may be counterproductive when treating students with mental health problems.

Because of the variation of models of collaboration from campus to campus, the ACHA Task Force essentially concludes by recommending that careful thought and consideration be given to any proposal to merge or integrate the two services. Many colleges appear to have good working relationships between the two units without ever having to merge their services (ACHA, 2010).

Summary and Final Thoughts

As we begin the early part of a new decade, it appears that the future of college counseling faces many uncertainties. College counselors seem poised to move forward despite lingering concerns about the prospect of outsourcing, charging fees for their services, increasing use of psychiatric services, and merging with health services. At a recent conference for college counselors who work in Pennsylvania's State System of Higher Education, the consensus seemed to be that all of the counseling centers were facing a high demand for services and more crisis- and emergency-oriented cases with only a limited amount of available resources. On the one hand, it was validating to know that this struggle was not unique and that college counselors at the other schools in the system were experiencing the same challenges. On the other hand, there was a sense of unease about the current state of affairs, particularly with the entire state system now facing a multimillion-dollar shortfall due to decreasing state appropriations. Some lamented about the changing nature of college counseling, suggesting that as resources continue to shrink, we may eventually transform into being campus crisis centers in which we will be primarily devoted to the prevention of suicide and homicide. This is certainly not the type of work that most college counselors originally signed up for when entering the field.

In many respects, it is not surprising that college counseling is quite different now than it was 20 or 30 years ago, just as it was quite different back then compared to 20 or 30 years before that. A certain percentage of college counselors in earlier times may have been concerned about the movement toward doing more personal counseling after primarily doing vocational counseling. But college counselors have evolved along with the changes in the larger culture. Perhaps one of the great strengths of the profession has been the resiliency of college counselors to adapt to the changing nature of the times and characteristics of the students they serve to provide the quality of services needed. There is a sense of hope and optimism that the profession will meet all of the current challenges and continue to flourish as a vital and integral part of campus life.

Back in the 1990s, college counselors discussed how counseling services tended to be viewed as an important resource for students, but not so much in a visible way. Some noted, for example, that on tours given for prospective students, no mention was ever made of counseling even as tour guides commented on all other services housed in the same building with counseling services. These tours tended to focus attention on the things assumed to be of most interest to prospective students, such as the fast food outlets and recreational facilities on campus. How many students, after all, really wanted to know about the availability of counseling services as part of their decision to choose a particular school? Many of today's students, if asked, might still find it more appealing to have a Starbucks on campus rather than counseling services. However, this sentiment may be undergoing a change among current and prospective students who increasingly come to understand the value of having access to quality counseling services on campus when needed.

In closing, it can be important to revisit the primary goal for writing this book. This book was intended to provide a thorough understanding of the many roles, responsibilities, contributions, and unique challenges of college counselors on campuses today. Hence, regardless of the reader's background and specific reason for reading this book, it is hoped that from doing so the reader has not only a better understanding of the profession of college counseling but a greater appreciation for the profession as well.

References

Affsprung, E. H. (2010). Legal action taken against college and university counseling centers 1986–2008. *Journal of College Student Psychotherapy*, *24*, 130–138.

Alexitch, L. R. (2006). Help seeking and the role of academic advising in higher education. In S. A. Karabanick & R. S. Newman (Eds.), *Help seeking in academic settings: Goals, groups, and contexts* (pp. 175–202). Mahwah, NJ: Lawrence Erlbaum.

Amada, G. (1992). Coping with the disruptive college student: A practical model. *Journal of American College Health*, *40*, 203–215.

Amada, G. (1993). The role of the mental health consultant in dealing with disruptive college students. *Journal of College Student Psychotherapy*, *8*, 121–137.

Amada, G. (1994). *Coping with the disruptive college student: A practical model.* Asheville, NC: College Administration Publications.

Amada, G. (1997). The disruptive college student: Recent trends and practical advice. *Journal of College Student Psychotherapy*, *11*, 57–67.

Amada, G. (1999). Disqualifying specified students from the campus psychological service: Some considerations and guidelines. *Journal of College Student Psychotherapy*, *13*, 7–24.

Amada, G. (2007). The massacre at Virginia Polytechnic Institute and State University: Some thoughts and considerations. *Journal of College Student Psychotherapy*, *22*, 3–11.

American College Counseling Association, Community College Task Force. (2009–2010). *2009–2010 community college counselors survey.* Retrieved February 14, 2011, from http://www.collegecounseling.org/community-college-survey-09–10

American College Health Association, Mental Health Best Practices Task Force. (2010). Considerations for integration of counseling and health services on college and university campuses. *Journal of American College Health, 58*, 583–596.

American Counseling Association. (2005). *ACA code of ethics*. Alexandria, VA: Author.

American Psychiatric Association. (2000). *Diagnostic and statistical manual of mental disorders* (4th ed., text rev.). Washington, DC: Author.

American Psychological Association. (2000). *Guidelines for psychotherapy with lesbian, gay, and bisexual clients*. Washington, DC: Author.

American Psychological Association. (2002). Ethical principles of psychologists and code of conduct. *American Psychologist, 57*, 1060–1073.

American Psychological Association. (2003). Guidelines on multicultural education, training, research, practice, and organizational change for psychologists. *American Psychologist, 58*, 377–402.

American Psychological Association, Committee on Accreditation. (2007). *Guidelines and principles for accreditation of programs in professional psychology*. Retrieved April 20, 2010, from http://apa.org/ed/accreditation/about/policies/guiding-principles.pdf

American Psychological Association, Office of Ethnic Minority Affairs. (1991). *Guidelines for providers of psychological services to ethnic, linguistic, and culturally diverse populations*. Washington, DC: Author.

Appelbaum, P. S. (2006). "Depressed? Get out!": Dealing with suicidal students on college campuses. *Psychiatric Services, 57*, 914–916.

Archer, J., Jr. (1992). Campus in crisis: Coping with fear and panic related to serial murders. *Journal of Counseling and Development, 71*, 96–100.

Arenson, K. W. (2004, December 3). Worried colleges step up efforts over suicide. *New York Yimes*, p. 1.

Arnett, J. J. (2000). Emerging adulthood: A theory of development from the late teens through the twenties. *American Psychologist, 55*, 469–480.

Arredondo, P., Toporek, R., Brown, S. P., Jones, J., Locke, D. C., Sanchez, J., & Stadler, H. (1996). Operationalization of the multicultural counseling competencies. *Journal of Multicultural Counseling and Development, 24*, 42–78.

Association for Counselor Education and Supervision. (1993). *ACES ethical guidelines for counseling supervisors*. Retrieved April 10, 2010, from http://www.acesonline.net/ethical_guidelines.asp

Association of Psychology Postdoctoral and Internship Centers. (2006). *APPIC membership criteria: Doctoral psychology internship programs*. Retrieved April 20, 2010, from http://www.appic.org/about/2_3_1_about_policies_and_procedures_internship.html

Backels, K., & Wheeler, I. (2001). Faculty perceptions of mental health issues among college students. *Journal of College Student Development, 42*, 173–176.

Baker, T. R. (2005). Notifying parents following a college student suicide attempt: A review of case law and FERPA, and recommendations for practice. *NASPA Journal, 42*, 513–533.

Baker, T. R. (2006). Parents of suicidal college students: What deans, judges, and legislators should know about campus research findings. *NASPA Journal, 43*, 164–181.

Barnette, V. (2006). A scholarly work commitment in practice. *Counselling Psychology Quarterly, 19*, 253–263.

Baron, J. (1988). Use of family psychotherapy techniques on the college campus. *Journal of College Student Psychotherapy, 3*, 83–96.

Baron, J., Bierschwale, D., & Bleiberg, J. R. (2006). Clinical implications of students' use of online communication for college psychotherapy. *Journal of College Student Psychotherapy, 20*, 69–77.

Barr, V., Rando, R., Krylowicz, B., & Winfield, E. (2010). *The Association for University and College Counseling Center Directors (AUCCCD) annual survey*. Retrieved May 10, 2010, from www.aucccd.org

Beamish, P. M. (2005). Introduction to the special section—Severe and persistent mental illness on college campuses: Considerations for service provision. *Journal of College Counseling, 8*, 138–139.

Beecher, M. E., Preece, J. E., & Roberts, N. L. (2007). Achieving accessible counseling for students with mobility impairments. In J. A. Lippincott & R. B. Lippincott (Eds.), *Special populations in college counseling: A handbook for mental health professionals* (pp. 203–217). Alexandria, VA: American Counseling Association.

Beecher, M. E., Rabe, R. A., & Wilder, L. K. (2004). Practical guidelines for counseling students with disabilities. *Journal of College Counseling, 7*, 83–89.

Beilke, J. R., & Yssel, N. (1999). The chilly climate for students with disabilities in higher education. *College Student Journal, 33*, 364–371.

Beit-Hallahmi, B. (1974). Involving family members in student counseling. *Psychotherapy: Theory, Research, and Practice, 11*, 265–269.

Benshoff, J. M., & Bundy, A. P. (2000). Nontraditional college students. In D. C. Davis & K. M. Humphrey (Eds.), *College counseling: Issues and strategies for a new millennium* (pp. 133–151). Alexandria, VA: American Counseling Association.

Benton, S. A., Robertson, J. M., Tseng, W., Newton, F. B., & Benton, S. L. (2003). Changes in counseling center client problems across 13 years. *Professional Psychology: Research and Practice, 34*, 66–72.

Berg-Cross, L., & Green, R. (2010). The impact of the recession on college students. *Journal of College Student Psychotherapy, 24*, 2–16.

Berg-Cross, L., & Pak, V. (2006). Diversity issues. In P. A. Grayson & P. W. Meilman (Eds.), *College mental health practice* (pp. 153–172). New York: Brunner-Routledge.

Berger, C., Angera, J. J., Rawls, D. T., Rapaport, R. J., Bartels, E., & Black, R. J. (2002). College counseling centers with counselors in private practice: Guidelines to negotiate ethical challenges. *Journal of College Counseling*, 5, 99–104.

Bergin, J. W., & Bergin, J. J. (2007). The hidden disabilities: Counseling students with learning disabilities. In J. A. Lippincott & R. B. Lippincott (Eds.), *Special populations in college counseling: A handbook for mental health professionals* (pp. 259–272). Alexandria, VA: American Counseling Association.

Bernard, H. S., Roach, A. M., & Resnick, H. (1981). Training bartenders as helpers on a college campus. *Personnel and Guidance Journal*, 60, 119–121.

Berson, R. J. (1988). A bereavement group for college students. *Journal of American College Health*, 37, 101–108.

Birky, I., Sharkin, B. S., Marin, J., & Scappaticci, A. (1998). Confidentiality after referral: A study on how restrictions on disclosure affect relationships between therapists and referral sources. *Professional Psychology: Research and Practice*, 29, 179–182.

Bishop, J. B. (1990). The university counseling center: An agenda for the 1990s. *Journal of Counseling and Development*, 68, 408–413.

Bishop, J. B. (1995). Emerging administrative strategies for college and university counseling centers. *Journal of Counseling and Development*, 74, 33–38.

Bishop, J. B. (2002). Students with histories of counseling: Implications for counseling centers and other administrative units. *Journal of College Student Development*, 43, 130–133.

Bishop, J. B. (2006). College and university counseling centers: Questions in search of answers. *Journal of College Counseling*, 9, 6–19.

Bishop, J. B., Bishop, K. A., & Beale, C. L. (1992). A longitudinal look at faculty knowledge and perceptions of a university counseling center. *Journal of College Student Development*, 33, 374–375.

Bishop, J. B., Gallagher, R. P., & Cohen, D. (2000). College students' problems: Status, trends, and research. In D. C. Davis & K. M. Humphrey (Eds.), *College counseling: Issues and strategies for a new millennium* (pp. 89–110). Alexandria, VA: American Counseling Association.

Bishop, J. B., Lacour, M. A., Nutt, N. J., Yamada, V. A., & Lee, J. Y. (2004). Reviewing a decade of change in the student culture. *Journal of College Student Psychotherapy*, 18, 3–30.

Black, T., Westwood, M. J., & Sorsdal, M. N. (2007). From the front line to the front of the class: Counseling students who are military veterans. In J. A. Lippincott & R. B. Lippincott (Eds.), *Special populations in college counseling: A handbook for mental health professionals* (pp. 3–20). Alexandria, VA: American Counseling Association.

Booth, R. (1990). A short-term model for treating shyness in college students: A note on an exploratory study. *Psychological Reports*, 66, 417–418.

Boyd, V., Hattauer, E., Brandel, I. W., Buckles, N., Davidshofer, C., Deakin, S., Erskine, C., Hurley, G., Locher, L., Piorkowski, G., et al. (2003). Accreditation standards for university and college counseling centers. *Journal of Counseling and Development, 81*, 168–177.

Brackney, B. E., & Karabenick, S. A. (1995). Psychopathology and academic performance: The role of motivation and learning strategies. *Journal of Counseling Psychology, 42*, 456–465.

Bradley, L. J. (1995). Certification and licensure issues. *Journal of Counseling and Development, 74*, 185–186.

Bray, N. J., Braxton, J. M., & Sullivan, A. S. (1999). The influence of stress-related coping strategies on college student departure decisions. *Journal of College Student Development, 40*, 645–657.

Brilliant, J. J., & Gribben, C. A. (1993). A workshop for faculty and counselors on academic dishonesty. *Journal of College Student Development, 34*, 437–438.

Brinson, J. A., & Kottler, J. A. (1995a). International students in counseling: Some alternative models. *Journal of College Student Psychotherapy, 9*, 57–70.

Brinson, J. A., & Kottler, J. A. (1995b). Minorities' underutilization of counseling centers' mental health services: A case for outreach and consultation. *Journal of Mental Health Counseling, 17*, 371–386.

Brooks, D. K., Jr. (1996). The impact of credentialing on mental health counseling. In W. J. Weikel & A. J. Palmo (Eds.), *Foundations of mental health counseling* (pp. 259–275). Springfield, IL: Charles C Thomas.

Brown, S., Lipford Sanders, J., & Shaw, M. (1995). Kujichagulia: Uncovering the secrets of the heart; Group work with African American women on predominantly White campuses. *Journal for Specialists in Group Work, 20*, 151–158.

Browning, S., & Miron, P. (2007). Counseling students with autism and Asperger's syndrome: A primer for success as a social being and a student. In J. A. Lippincott & R. B. Lippincott (Eds.), *Special populations in college counseling: A handbook for mental health professionals* (pp. 273–285). Alexandria, VA: American Counseling Association.

Brunk, M. (1991). Applications of context to supervision in university counseling centers. *The Clinical Supervisor, 9*, 91–113.

Buelow, G., & Range, L. M. (2001). No-suicide contracts among college students. *Death Studies, 25*, 583–592.

Buhrke, R. A., & Stabb, S. D. (1995). Gay, lesbian, and bisexual student needs. In S. D. Stabb, S. M. Harris, & J. E. Talley (Eds.), *Multicultural needs assessment for college and university student populations* (pp. 173–201). Springfield, IL: Charles C Thomas.

Campus Care and Counseling Act, H.R. 3593, 108th Cong. (2003).

Campus Care and Counseling Act, S. 2215, 108th Cong. (2004).

Cardenas, J., Williams, K., Wilson, J. P., Fanouraki, G., & Singh, A. (2003). PTSD, major depressive symptoms, and substance abuse following September 11. 2001, in a midwestern university population. *International Journal of Emergency Mental Health, 5*, 15–28.

Carter, G. C., & Winseman, J. S. (2003). Increasing numbers of students arrive on college campuses on psychiatric medications: Are they mentally ill? *Journal of College Student Psychotherapy, 18*, 3–10.

Casey, D. (2004). Pre-crisis plans: The development of a crisis response team. In R. Lee & D. Casey (Eds.), *Crisis and trauma in colleges and universities* (pp. 89–103). Ellicott City, MD: Chevron Publishing.

Center for Collegiate Mental Health. (2009). *Counseling center assessment of psychological symptoms (CCAPS) user manual*. University Park: Pennsylvania State University.

Chickering, A. W., & Reisser, L. (1993). *Education and identity* (2nd ed.). San Francisco: Jossey-Bass.

Choate, L. H. (2003). Sexual assault prevention programs for college men: An exploratory evaluation of the Men Against Violence model. *Journal of College Counseling, 6*, 166–176.

Chojnacki, J., & Gelberg, S. (1995). The facilitation of a gay/lesbian, bisexual support therapy group by heterosexual counselors. *Journal of Counseling and Development, 73*, 352–354.

Christoffersen, J. (2011, April 2). U.S. reviews concerns on harassment at Yale. *The Boston Globe.* Retrieved April 3, 2011, from http://www.boston.com/news/local/connecticut/articles/2011/0402/us_reviews_concerns_on_harassment_at_yale/

Clark Oropeza, B. A., Fitzgibbon, M., & Baron, A., Jr. (1991). Managing mental health crises of foreign college students. *Journal of Counseling and Development, 69*, 280–284.

Coll, K. M. (1991). Mandatory psychiatric withdrawal from public colleges and universities: A review of potential legal violations and appropriate use. *Journal of College Student Psychotherapy, 5*, 91–98.

Coll, K. M. (1995). Clinical supervision of community college counselors: Current and preferred practices. *Counselor Education and Supervision, 35*, 111–117.

Constantine, M. G., Chen, E. C., & Ceesay, P. (1997). Intake concerns of racial and ethnic minority students at a university counseling center: Implications for developmental programming and outreach. *Journal of Multicultural Counseling and Development, 25*, 210–218.

Constantine, M. G., Wilton, L., & Caldwell, L. D. (2003). The role of social support in moderating the relationship between psychological distress and willingness to seek psychological help among Black and Latino college students. *Journal of College Counseling, 6*, 155–165.

Cooper, S. E. (2005). Evidence-based psychotherapy practice in college mental health. *Journal of College Student Psychotherapy, 20*, 1–6.

Cooper, S. E., & Archer, J. A., Jr. (2002). Evaluation and research in college counseling center contexts. *Journal of College Counseling, 5*, 50–59.

Cooper, S. E., Resnick, J. L., Rodolfa, E., & Douce, L. (2008). College counseling and mental health services: A 20-year perspective of issues and challenges. In B. W. Walsh (Ed.), *Biennial review of counseling psychology* (Vol. 1, pp. 209–230). New York: Routledge/Taylor & Francis Group.

Cornell, D. (2008). Threat assessment on the college campus. *Leadership Exchange, 5*, 8–14.

Cornish, J. A., Kominars, K. D., Riva, M. T., McIntosh, S., & Henderson, M. C. (2000). Perceived distress in university counseling center clients across a six-year period. *Journal of College Student Development, 41*, 104–109.

Corrigan, M. J., Jones, C. A., & McWhirter, J. J. (2001). College students with disabilities: An access employment group. *Journal for Specialists in Group Work, 26*, 339–349.

Coulter, L. P., Offutt, C. A., & Mascher, J. (2003). Counseling center management of after-hours crises: Practice and problems. *Journal of College Student Psychotherapy, 18*, 11–34.

Cutler, H. A. (2003). Parental notification and family counseling: Amendments to FERPA. *The Family Journal: Counseling and Therapy for Couples and Families, 11*, 174–177.

Dale, K. A., & Alpert, J. L. (2006). New York University and 9/11: Viewing terrorism through a dormitory window. In L. Barbanel & R. J. Sternberg (Eds.), *Psychological interventions in times of crisis* (pp. 119–132). New York: Springer.

Damer, D. E., Latimer, K. M., & Porter, S. H. (2010). "Build your social confidence": A social anxiety group for college students. *Journal for Specialists in Group Work, 35*, 7–22.

Dannells, M., & Stuber, D. (1992). Mandatory psychiatric withdrawal of severely disturbed students: A study and policy recommendations. *NASPA Journal, 29*, 163–168.

D'Augelli, A. R. (1992). Lesbian and gay male undergraduates' experiences of harassment and fear on campus. *Journal of Interpersonal Violence, 7*, 383–395.

D'Augelli, A. R. (1993). Preventing mental health problems among lesbian and gay college students. *Journal of Primary Prevention, 13*, 245–261.

D'Augelli, A. R., & Rose, M. L. (1990). Homophobia in a university community: Attitudes and experiences of heterosexual freshmen. *Journal of College Student Development, 31*, 484–491.

Daughhetee, C. (2001). Using genograms as a tool for insight in college counseling. *Journal of College Counseling, 4*, 73–76.

Davenport, R. (2009). From college counselor to "risk manager": The evolving nature of college counseling on today's campuses. *Journal of American College Health, 58*, 181–183.

Davidson, M. M., Yakushka, O. F., & Sanford-Martens, T. C. (2004). Racial and ethnic minority clients' utilization of a university counseling center: An archival study. *Journal of Multicultural Counseling and Development, 32*, 259–271.

Davis, H., Jr., Kocet, M. M., & Zozone, M. S. (2001). Counselor-in-residence: Counseling service model for residential college students. *Journal of College Counseling, 4,* 190–192.

Davis, J. M., Bates, C., & Velasquez, R. J. (1990). Faculty suicide: Guidelines for effective coping with a suicide in a counselor training program. *Counselor Education and Supervision, 29,* 197–204.

Dean, L. A. (2000). College counseling today: Changing roles and definitions. In D. C. Davis & K. M. Humphrey (Eds.), *College counseling: Issues and strategies for a new millennium* (pp. 41–70). Alexandria, VA: American Counseling Association.

Dean, L. A., & Meadows, M. E. (1995). College counseling: Union and inter-section. *Journal of Counseling and Development, 74,* 139–142.

De Lucia, R. C., & Iasenza, S. (1995). Student disruption, disrespect, and disorder in class: A seminar for faculty. *Journal of College Student Development, 36,* 385–388.

DeRoma, V., Saylor, C., Swickert, R., Sinisi, C., Marable, T. B., & Vickery, P. (2003). College students' PTSD symptoms, coping, and perceived benefits following media exposure to 9/11. *Journal of College Student Psychotherapy, 18,* 49–64.

Dinklage, K. T. (1991). Counseling the learning disabled college student. *Journal of College Student Psychotherapy, 5,* 3–27.

DiScala, J., Olswang, S. G., & Niccolls, C. S. (1992). College and university responses to the emotionally and mentally impaired student. *Journal of College and University Law, 19,* 17–33.

Doumas, D. M., & Anderson, L. L. (2009). Reducing alcohol use in first-year university students: Evaluation of a web-based personalized feedback program. *Journal of College Counseling, 12,* 18–32.

Downey, J. P., & Stage, F. K. (1999). Hate crime and violence on college and university campuses. *Journal of College Student Development, 40,* 3–9.

Draper, M. R., Jennings, J., Baron, A., Erdur, O., & Shankar, L. (2002). Time-limited counseling outcome in a nationwide college counseling center sample. *Journal of College Counseling, 5,* 26–38.

Drum, D. J., Brownson, C., Denmark, A. B., & Smith, S. E. (2009). New data on the nature of suicidal crises in college settings: Shifting the paradigm. *Professional Psychology: Research and Practice, 40,* 213–222.

Ducey, C. P. (2006). Academic difficulties. In P. A. Grayson & P. W. Meilman (Eds.), *College mental health practice* (pp. 173–193). New York: Brunner-Routledge.

Duenwald, M. (2004, October 26). The dorms may be great, but how's the counseling? *New York Times.* Retrieved October 28, 2004, from http://www.nytimes.com/2004/10/26/health/psychology/26cons.html

Dworkin, J. (2005). Risk taking as developmentally appropriate experimenta-tion for college students. *Journal of Adolescent Research, 20,* 219–241.

Eaves, C. (2001). The development and implementation of a crisis response team in a school setting. *International Journal of Emergency Mental Health, 3,* 35–46.

Eells, G. T., Seals, T., Rockett, J., & Hayes, D. (2005). Enjoying the roller coaster ride: Directors' perspectives on fostering staff morale in university counseling centers. *Journal of College Student Psychotherapy, 20,* 17–28.

Ellingson, K. T., Kochenour, E. O., & Weitzman, L. M. (1999). University counseling center consultation: Developing a faculty outreach program. *Consulting Psychology Journal: Practice and Research, 51,* 31–36.

Ender, S. C., & Newton, F. B. (2000). *Students helping students: A guide for peer educators on campuses.* San Francisco: Jossey-Bass.

Evans, N. J., & Broido, E. M. (2002). The experiences of lesbian and bisexual women in college residence halls: Implications for addressing homophobia and heterosexism. *Journal of Lesbian Studies, 6,* 29–42.

Fabiano, P., Perkins, W., Berkowitz, A., Linkenbach, J., & Stark, C. (2003). Engaging men as social justice allies in ending violence against women: Evidence for a social norms approach. *Journal of American College Health, 52,* 105–112.

Fulvey, J. E. (2002). *Managing clinical supervision: Ethical practice and legal risk management.* Pacific Grove, CA: Brooks/Cole.

Farrell, E. F. (2004, October 8). Asperger's confounds colleges: A surge of students with an autism-related disorder poses new challenges. *The Chronicle of Higher Education, 51,* p. A35.

Flynn, C., & Heitzmann, D. (2008). Tragedy at Virginia Tech: Trauma and its aftermath. *The Counseling Psychologist, 36,* 479–489.

Foreman, M. E. (1990). The counselor's assessment and intervention with the suicidal student. *Journal of College Student Psychotherapy, 4,* 125–140.

Francis, P. C. (2000). Practicing ethically as a college counselor. In D. C. Davis & K. M. Humphrey (Eds.), *College counseling: Issues and strategies for a new millennium* (pp. 71–86). Alexandria, VA: American Counseling Association.

Francis, P. C. (2003). Developing ethical institutional policies and procedures for working with suicidal students on a college campus. *Journal of College Counseling, 6,* 114–123.

Francis, P. C. (2009). Counseling issues in college students. In I. Marini & M. A. Stebnicki (Eds.), *The professional counselor's desk reference* (pp. 747–756). New York: Springer.

Franke, A. H. (2004, June 25). When students kill themselves, colleges may get the blame. *The Chronicle of Higher Education, 50,* p. B18.

Fromm, M. G. (2007). The escalating use of medications by college students: What are they telling us, what are we telling them? *Journal of College Student Psychotherapy, 21,* 27–44.

Fukuyama, M. A., & Delgado-Romero, E. A. (2003). Against the odds: Successfully implementing multicultural counseling competencies in a counseling center on a predominantly White campus. In G. Roysircar, D. S. Sandhu, & V. E. Bibbins (Eds.), *Multicultural competencies: A guidebook of practices* (pp. 205–216). Alexandria, VA: Association for Multicultural Counseling and Development.

Furr, S. R., Westefeld, J. S., McConnell, G. N., & Jenkins, J. M. (2001). Suicide and depression among college students: A decade later. *Professional Psychology: Research and Practice, 32,* 97–100.

Gage, L. A., & Gyorky, Z. K. (1990). Identifying appropriate clients for time-limited counseling. *Journal of College Student Development, 31,* 476–477.

Gallagher, R. P. (2009). *National survey of counseling center directors.* Retrieved March 20, 2010, from http://www.iacsinc.org/2009%20National%20Survey.pdf

Gallagher, R. P. (2010). *National survey of counseling center directors.* Retrieved February 1, 2011, from http://www.iacsinc.org/NSCCD%202010.pdf

Gallessich, J., & Olmstead, K. M. (1987). Training in counseling psychology: Issues and trends in 1986. *The Counseling Psychologist, 15,* 596–600.

Garlow, S. J., Rosenberg, J., Moore, J. D., Haas, A. P., Koestner, B., Hendlin, H., & Nemeroff, C. B. (2008). Depression, desperation, and suicidal ideation in college students: Results from the American Foundation for Suicide Prevention College Screening Project at Emory University. *Depression and Anxiety, 25,* 482–488.

Garrett Lee Smith Memorial Act, H.R. 4799, 108th Cong. (2004).

Garrett Lee Smith Memorial Act, S. 2674, 108th Cong. (2004).

Gary, J. M. (2007). Counseling adult learners: Individual interventions, group interventions, and campus resources. In J. A. Lippincott & R. B. Lippincott (Eds.), *Special populations in college counseling: A handbook for mental health professionals* (pp. 99–113). Alexandria, VA: American Counseling Association.

Ghetie, D. (2007). The debate over time-limited treatment in college counseling centers. *Journal of College Student Psychotherapy, 22,* 41–61.

Gibson, J. M. (2000). Documentation of emotional and mental disabilities: The role of the counseling center. *Journal of College Counseling, 3,* 63–72.

Gilbert, S. P. (1989). The juggling act of the college counseling center: A point of view. *The Counseling Psychologist, 17,* 477–489.

Gilbert, S. P. (1992). Ethical issues in the treatment of severe psychopathology in university and college counseling centers. *Journal of Counseling and Development, 70,* 695–699.

Gintner, G. G., & Choate, L. H. (2007). Counseling students who are problem drinkers: Screening, assessment, and intervention. In J. A. Lippincott & R. B. Lippincott (Eds.), *Special populations in college counseling: A handbook for mental health professionals* (pp. 157–171). Alexandria, VA: American Counseling Association.

Golden, B. R., Corazzini, J. G., & Grady, P. (1993). Current practices of group therapy at university counseling centers: A national survey. *Professional Psychology: Research and Practice, 24,* 228–230.

Goode, E. (2003, February 3). More in college seek help for psychological problems. *New York Times,* p. A11.

Grayson, P. A. (1986). Mental health confidentiality on the small campus. *Journal of American College Health, 34,* 187–191.

Grayson, P. A., & Meilman, P. W. (Eds.). (2006). *College mental health practice.* New York: Brunner-Routledge.

Greer, T. M., & White, A. M. (2008). Women of color groups: Group counseling with African American college women. In L. Vandecreek & J. B. Allen (Eds.), *Innovations in clinical practice: Focus on groups, couples, and family therapy* (pp. 253–264). Sarasota, FL: Professional Resource Press/ Professional Resource Exchange.

Grieger, I., & Toliver, S. (2001). Multiculturalism on predominantly White campuses: Multiple roles and functions for the counselor. In J. G. Ponterotto, J. M. Casas, L. A. Suzuki, & C. M. Alexander (Eds.), *Handbook of multicultural counseling* (pp. 825–848). Thousand Oaks, CA: Sage.

Guinee, J. P., & Ness, M. E. (2000). Counseling centers of the 1990s: Challenges and changes. *The Counseling Psychologist, 28*, 267–280.

Gyorky, Z. K., Royalty, G. M., & Johnson, D. H. (1994). Time-limited therapy in university counseling centers: Do time-limited and time-unlimited centers differ? *Professional Psychology: Research and Practice, 25*, 50–54.

Haines, M. E., Norris, M. P., & Kashy, D. A. (1996). The effects of depressed mood on academic performance in college students. *Journal of College Student Development, 37*, 519–526.

Halstead, R. W., & Derbort, J. J. (1988). Counselor-in-residence: A proactive and early intervention program for delivery of counseling services. *Journal of College Student Development, 29*, 378–379.

Hansen, D. G. (1999). Key factors that differentiate nontraditional from traditional students. In Y. M. Jenkins (Ed.), *Diversity in college settings: Directives for helping professionals* (pp. 191–199). New York: Routledge.

Hargrove, D. S., McDaniel, S. H., Malone, E., & Christiansen, M. D. (2006). Family problems. In P. A. Grayson & P. W. Meilman (Eds.), *College mental health practice* (pp. 79–93). New York: Brunner-Routledge.

Harris, H. L., Altekruse, M. K., & Engels, D. W. (2003). Helping freshman student athletes adjust to college life using psychoeducational groups. *Journal for Specialists in Group Work, 28*, 64–81.

Harris, R. S. (2002). Dual relationships and university counseling center environments. In A. A. Lazarus & O. Zur (Eds.), *Dual relationships and psychotherapy* (pp. 337–347). New York: Springer.

Harris, R. S., Aldea, M. A., & Kirkley, D. E. (2006). A motivational interviewing and common factors approach to change in working with alcohol use and abuse in college students. *Professional Psychology: Research and Practice, 37*, 614–621.

Harris, S. (1994). The counselor-in-residence program. *Journal of College Student Development, 35*, 140.

Hatchett, G. T. (2004). Reducing premature termination in university counseling centers. *Journal of College Student Psychotherapy, 19*, 13–27.

Hayes, B. G., Freeman, M. S., Vogel, J. E., Clonch, M., Clarke, N., & Duffey, T. (2008). Destigmatizing college counseling for first-year students: A psychodrama approach. *Journal of College Student Development, 49*, 250–254.

Hayman, P. M., & Covert, J. A. (1986). Ethical dilemmas in college counseling centers. *Journal of Counseling and Development, 64*, 318–320.

Hernandez, T. J., & Fister, D. L. (2001). Dealing with disruptive and emotional college students: A systems model. *Journal of College Counseling, 4,* 49–62.

Herr, E. L., Heitzmann, D. E., & Rayman, J. R. (2006). *The professional counselor as administrator: Perspectives on leadership and management in counseling services across settings.* Mahwah, NJ: Lawrence Erlbaum.

Hinkelman, J. M. (2005). University counseling center: Bridging the gap between university counseling centers and academia. In R. D. Morgan, T. L. Kuther, & C. J. Habben (Eds.), *Life after graduate school in psychology: Insider's advice from new psychologists* (pp. 73–85). New York: Psychology Press.

Hinkelman, J. M., & Luzzo, D. A. (2007). Mental health and career development of college students. *Journal of Counseling and Development, 85,* 143–147.

Hipple, J., & Beamish, P. M. (2007). Supervision of counselor trainees with clients in crisis. *Journal of Professional Counseling: Practice, Theory, and Research, 35,* 1–16.

Hodges, S. (2001). University counseling centers at the twenty-first century: Looking forward, looking back. *Journal of College Counseling, 4,* 161–173.

Hosie, T. W. (1995). Counseling specialties: A case of basic preparation rather than advanced specialization. *Journal of Counseling and Development, 74,* 177–180.

Hunter, B., & Lowery, J. W. (2008). Campus safety and the Clery Act. *Leadership Exchange, 5,* 34–35.

Iosupovici, M., & Luke, E. (2002). College and university student counseling centers: Inevitable boundary shifts and dual roles. In A. A. Lazarus & O. Zur (Eds.), *Dual relationships and psychotherapy* (pp. 360–378). New York: Springer.

Jackson, K. (2009). The use of family therapy within a university counseling center. *Journal of College Student Psychotherapy, 23,* 253–261.

Javorsky, J., & Gussin, B. (1994). College students with attention deficit hyperactivity disorder: An overview and description of services. *Journal of College Student Development, 35,* 170–177.

Jenkins, Y. M. (1999). Diversity in college settings. In Y. M. Jenkins (Ed.), *Diversity in college settings: Directives for helping professionals* (pp. 5–20). New York: Routledge.

Johnson, L. R., & Sandhu, D. S. (2007). Isolation, adjustment, and acculturation issues of international students: Intervention strategies for counselors. In H. D. Singaravelu & M. Pope (Eds.), *A handbook for counseling international students in the United States* (pp. 13–35). Alexandria, VA: American Counseling Association.

Jurgens, J. C., Schwitzer, A. M., & Middleton, T. (2004). Examining attitudes toward college students with minority sexual orientations: Findings and suggestions. *Journal of College Student Psychotherapy, 19,* 57–75.

Kadison, R. D., & DiGeronimo, T. F. (2004). *College of the overwhelmed: The campus mental health crisis and what to do about it.* San Francisco: Jossey-Bass.

Kandell, J. J. (1998). Internet addiction on campus: The vulnerability of college students. *Cyberpsychology and Behavior, 1*, 11–17.

Kaslow, N. J., & Echols, M. M. (2006). Postdoctoral training and requirements for licensure and certification. In T. J. Vaughn (Ed.), *Psychology licensure and certification: What students need to know* (pp. 85–95). Washington, DC: American Psychological Association.

Kearney, L. K., Draper, M., & Baron, A. (2005). Counseling utilization by ethnic minority college students. *Cultural Diversity and Ethnic Minority Psychology, 11*, 272–285.

Kelly, B. T., & Torres, A. (2006). Campus safety: Perceptions and experiences of women students. *Journal of College Student Development, 47*, 20–36.

Kelly, K. (2001, January 15). Lost on the campus. *Time, 157*, 51–53.

Kennedy, A. (2004). NYU counseling director defends services, students in suicide media blitz. *Counseling Today, 46*, 28.

Kenney, K. (2007). Strategies and counselor competencies in counseling multiracial students. In J. A. Lippincott & R. B. Lippincott (Eds.), *Special populations in college counseling: A handbook for mental health professionals* (pp. 77–88). Alexandria, VA: American Counseling Association.

Kern, C. W. (2000). Outreach programming from the college counseling center. In D. C. Davis & K. M. Humphrey (Eds.), *College counseling: Issues and strategies for a new millennium* (pp. 205–219). Alexandria, VA: American Counseling Association.

Kessler, R. C., Foster, C. L., Saunders, W. B., & Stang, P. E. (1995). Social consequences of psychiatric disorders: Educational attainment. *American Journal of Psychiatry, 152*, 1026–1032.

Kettmann, J. D., Schoen, E. G., Moel, J. E., Cochran, S. V., Greenberg, S. T., & Corkery, J. M. (2007). Increasing severity of psychopathology at counseling centers: A new look. *Professional Psychology: Research and Practice, 38*, 523–529.

Kincade, E. A., & Kalodner, C. R. (2004). The use of groups in college and university counseling centers. In J. L. DeLucia-Waack, D. A. Gerrity, C. Kalodner, & M. T. Riva (Eds.), *Handbook of group counseling and psychotherapy* (pp. 366–377). Thousand Oaks, CA: Sage.

Kiracofe, N. M., & Buller, A. E. (2009). Mandated disciplinary counseling: Working effectively with challenging clients. *Journal of College Counseling, 12*, 71–84.

Kirn, W. (2003, November 3). University blues: A crisis. *Time, 162*, 55.

Kitzrow, M. A. (2003). The mental health needs of today's college students: Challenges and recommendations. *NASPA Journal, 41*, 165–179.

Kluger, J. (2003, November 3). Medicating young minds. *Time, 162*, 48–58.

Knox, D. (2007). Counseling students who are grieving: Finding meaning in loss. In J. A. Lippincott & R. B. Lippincott (Eds.), *Special populations in college counseling: A handbook for mental health professionals* (pp. 187–199). Alexandria, VA: American Counseling Association.

Koch, D. S. (2007). Counseling students who are visually impaired or blind. In J. A. Lippincott & R. B. Lippincott (Eds.), *Special populations in college counseling: A handbook for mental health professionals* (pp. 219–229). Alexandria, VA: American Counseling Association.

Lacour, M. A., & Carter, E. F. (2002). Challenges of referral decisions in college counseling. *Journal of College Student Psychotherapy, 17,* 39–52.

Lamb, C. S. (1992). Managing disruptive students: The mental health practitioner as a consultant for faculty and staff. *Journal of College Student Psychotherapy, 7,* 23–39.

Lance, L. M. (2002). Heterosexism and homophobia among college students. *College Student Journal, 36,* 410–414.

Lawe, C. F., Penick, J. M., Raskin, J. D., & Raymond, V. V. (1999). Influences on decisions to refer at university counseling centers. *Journal of College Student Psychotherapy, 14,* 59–68.

Leach, B. E., & Sewell, J. D. (1986). Responding to students with mental disorders: A framework for action. *NASPA Journal, 22,* 37–43.

Lederman, D. (1994, March 9). Weapons on campus: Officials warn that colleges are not immune from the scourge of handguns. *The Chronicle of Higher Education, 40,* p. A33.

Lee, D., Olson, E. A., Locke, B., Michelson, S. T., & Odes, E. (2009). The effects of college counseling services on academic performance and retention. *Journal of College Student Development, 50,* 305–319.

Lee, R. W., Caruso, M. E., Goins, S. E., & Southerland, J. P. (2003). Addressing sexual assault on college campuses: Guidelines for a prevention/awareness week. *Journal of College Counseling, 6,* 14–24.

Lenihan, G., & Kirk, W. G. (1990). Using student paraprofessionals in the treatment of eating disorders. *Journal of Counseling and Development, 68,* 332–335.

Levitt, R., & Candiotti, S. (2010, March 20). *Two suspected suicides confirmed at Cornell; Total now at six.* Retrieved March 22, 2010, from http://www.cnn.com/2010/US/03/20/new.york.cornell.suicides/index.html

Lin, J.-C. G. (2000). College counseling and international students. In D. C. Davis & K. M. Humphrey (Eds.), *College counseling: Issues and strategies for a new millennium* (pp. 169–183). Alexxandria, VA: American Counseling Association.

Lindsey, B. J. (1997). Peer education: A viewpoint and critique. *Journal of American College Health, 45,* 187–189.

Lippincott, J. A., & German, N. (2007). From blue collar to ivory tower: Counseling first-generation, working class students. In J. A. Lippincott & R. B. Lippincott (Eds.), *Special populations in college counseling: A handbook for mental health professionals* (pp. 89–98). Alexandria, VA: American Counseling Association.

Lippincott, J. A., & Lippincott, R. B. (Eds.). (2007). *Special populations in college counseling: A handbook for mental health professionals.* Alexandria, VA: American Counseling Association.

Luepker, E. T. (2003). *Record keeping in psychotherapy and counseling: Protecting confidentiality and the professional relationship.* New York: Brunner-Routledge.

Malley, P., Gallagher, R., & Brown, S. M. (1992). Ethical problems in university and college counseling centers: A Delphi study. *Journal of College Student Development, 33*, 238–244.

Maples, M. (2000). Professional preparation for college counseling: Quality assurance. In D. C. Davis & K. M. Humphrey (Eds.), *College counseling: Issues and strategies for a new millennium* (pp. 57–70). Alexandria, VA: American Counseling Association.

Marks, L. I., & McLaughlin, R. H. (2005). Outreach by college counselors: Increasing student attendance at presentations. *Journal of College Counseling, 8*, 86–96.

Mathewson, R. H. (1946). The advisement of veterans at college and university centers: First appraisal. *American Psychologist, 1*, 201–204.

May, R. (2000). Basic requirements and survival strategies for a college psychotherapy service. *Journal of College Student Psychotherapy, 15*, 3–13.

McCarthy, M. A., & Butler, L. (2003). Responding to traumatic events on college campuses: A case study and assessment of student postdisaster anxiety. *Journal of College Counseling, 6*, 90–96.

McEneaney, A. M., & Gross, J. M. (2009). Introduction to the special issue: Group interventions in college counseling centers. *International Journal of Group Psychotherapy, 59*, 455–460.

McGinn, D., & DePasquale, R. (2004, August 23). Taking depression on. *Newsweek, 144*, pp. 59–60.

Meadows, M. E. (2000). The evolution of college counseling. In D. C. Davis & K. M. Humphrey (Eds.), *College counseling: Issues and strategies for a new millennium* (pp. 15–40). Alexandria, VA: American Counseling Association.

Meilman, P. W., & Gaylor, M. S. (1989). Substance abuse. In P. A. Grayson & K. Cauley (Eds.), *College psychotherapy* (pp. 193–215). New York: Guilford.

Meilman, P. W., Hacker, D. S., & Kraus-Zeilmann, D. (1993). Use of the mental health on-call system on a university campus. *Journal of American College Health, 42*, 105–109.

Meilman, P. W., & Hall, T. M. (2006). Aftermath of tragic events: The development and use of community support meetings on a university campus. *Journal of American College Health, 54*, 382–384.

Meilman, P. W., Leichliter, J. S., & Presley, C. A. (1998). Analysis of weapon carrying among college students, by region and institution type. *Journal of American College Health, 46*, 291–299.

Meilman, P. W., Lewis, D. K., & Gerstein, L. (2006). Alcohol, drugs, and other addictions. In P. A. Grayson & P. W. Meilman (Eds.), *College mental health practice* (pp. 195–214). New York: Brunner-Routledge.

Meilman, P. W., Manley, C., Gaylor, M. S., & Turco, J. H. (1992). Medical withdrawals from college for mental health reasons and their relation to academic performance. *Journal of American College Health, 40*, 217–223.

Meilman, P. W., Pattis, J. A., & Kraus-Zeilmann, D. (1994). Suicide attempts and threats on one college campus: Policy and practice. *Journal of American College Health, 42*, 147–154.

Mellott, R. N. (2007). The scientist-practitioner training model for professional psychology. *American Behavioral Scientist, 50*, 755–757.

Mental Health on Campus Improvement Act, H.R. 1704, 111th Cong. (2009).

Mental Health on Campus Improvement Act, S. 682, 111th Cong. (2009).

Mier, S., Boone, M., & Shropshire, S. (2009). Community consultation and intervention: Supporting students who do not access counseling services. *Journal of College Student Psychotherapy, 23*, 16–29.

Miller, K. L., Miller, S. M., & Evans, W. J. (2002). Computer-assisted live supervision in college counseling centers. *Journal of College Counseling, 5*, 187–192.

Miller, M., Hemenway, D., & Wechsler, H. (2002). Guns and gun threats at college. *Journal of American College Health, 51*, 57–65.

Millon, T., Strack, S., Millon-Niedbala, M., & Grossman, S. D. (2008). Using the Millon College Counseling Inventory to assess student mental health needs. *Journal of College Counseling, 11*, 159–172.

Mitchell, R. W. (2007). *Documentation in counseling records: An overview of ethical, legal and clinical issues* (3rd ed.). Alexandria, VA: American Counseling Association.

Mitchell, S. L., Elmore, K., & Fygetakis, L. M. (1996). A coordinated campus response to student suicide. *Journal of College Student Development, 37*, 698–699.

Mori, S. (2000). Addressing the mental health concerns of international students. *Journal of Counseling and Development, 78*, 137–144.

Much, K., & Swanson, A. L. (2010). The debate about increasing college student psychopathology: Are college students really getting "sicker"? *Journal of College Student Psychotherapy, 24*, 86–97.

Much, K., Wagener, A. M., & Hellenbrand, M. (2010). Practicing in the 21st century college counseling center. *Journal of College Student Psychotherapy, 24*, 32–38.

Munley, P. H., Duncan, L. E., McDonnell, K. A., & Sauer, E. M. (2004). Counseling psychology in the United States of America. *Counselling Psychology Quarterly, 17*, 247–271.

Murphy, M. C., & Martin, T. L. (2004). Introducing a team-based clinical intake system at a university counseling center: A good method for handling client demand. *Journal of College Student Psychotherapy, 19*, 3–12.

Mustaine, B. L., West, P. L., & Wyrick, B. K. (2003). Substance abuse counselor certification requirements: Is it time for a change? *Journal of Addictions and Offender Counseling, 23*, 99–107.

National Center for Higher Education Risk Management. (2010). *College and university behavioral intervention team model.* Retrieved May 5, 2010, from http://www.ncherm.org/cubit.html

Neil, M. (2010, January 13). Judge OKs duty-to-warn suits in Va. Tech shootings, nixes immunity claim. *ABA Journal*. Retrieved January 14, 2010, from http://www.abajournal.com/news/article/judge_rejects_immunity_claim_oks_duty-to-warn_suits_in_va._tech_shootings/

Neimeyer, G. J., Bowman, J., & Stewart, A. E. (2001). Internship and initial job placements in counseling psychology: A 26-year retrospective. *The Counseling Psychologist, 29*, 763–780.

Newton, F. B. (1990). Academic support seminars: A program to assist students experiencing academic difficulty. *Journal of College Student Development, 31*, 183–186.

Nilsson, J. E., Berkel, L. A., Flores, L. Y., & Lucas, M. S. (2004). Utilization rate and presenting concerns of international students at a university counseling center: Implications for outreach programming. *Journal of College Student Psychotherapy, 19*, 49–59.

Nishimura, N. J. (1998). Assessing the issues of multiracial students on college campuses. *Journal of College Counseling, 1*, 45–53.

Nolan, J. M., Ford, S. J. W., Kress, V. E., Anderson, R. I., & Novak, T. C. (2005). A comprehensive model for addressing severe and persistent mental illness on campuses: The New Diversity Initiative. *Journal of College Counseling, 8*, 172–179.

Nolan, J. M., Levy, E. G., & Constantine, M. G. (1996). Meeting the developmental needs of diverse students: The impact of a peer education program. *Journal of College Student Development, 37*, 588–589.

Nolan, S. A., Pace, K. A., Iannelli, R. J., Palma, T. V., & Pakalns, G. P. (2006). A simple and effective program to increase faculty knowledge of and referrals to counseling centers. *Journal of College Counseling, 9*, 167–170.

O'Malley, K., Wheeler, I., Murphey, J., O'Connell, J., & Waldo, M. (1990). Changes in levels of psychopathology being treated at college and university counseling centers. *Journal of College Student Development, 31*, 464–465.

O'Neill, D. J., & Fontaine, G. D. (1973). Counseling for the Vietnam veteran. *Journal of College Student Personnel, 14*, 153–155.

Osborn, C. J., & Davis, T. E. (1996). The supervision contract: Making it perfectly clear. *The Clinical Supervisor, 14*, 121–134.

Owen, J., Devdas, L., & Rodolfa, E. (2007). University counseling center off-campus referrals: An exploratory investigation. *Journal of College Student Psychotherapy, 22*, 13–29.

Owen, J., Smith, A., & Rodolfa, E. (2009). Clients' expected number of counseling sessions, treatment effectiveness, and termination status: Using empirical evidence to inform session limit policies. *Journal of College Student Psychotherapy, 23*, 118–134.

Owen, J., Tao, K. W., & Rodolfa, E. R. (2005). Supervising counseling center trainees in the era of evidence-based practice. *Journal of College Student Psychotherapy, 20*, 67–77.

Page, R. C., & Bailey, J. B. (1995). Addictions counseling certification: An emerging counseling specialty. *Journal of Counseling and Development, 74,* 167–171.

Paladino, D. A. (2009). Counseling multiple heritage college students. In R. C. Henriksen, Jr. & D. A. Paladino (Eds.), *Counseling multiple heritage individuals, couples, and families* (pp. 83–100). Alexandria, VA: American Counseling Association.

Paladino, D. A., & Davis, H., Jr. (2006). Counseling and outreach strategies for assisting multiracial college students. *Journal of College Student Psychotherapy, 20,* 19–31.

Palma, T. V., & Stanley, J. L. (2002). Effective counseling with lesbian, gay, and bisexual clients. *Journal of College Counseling, 5,* 74–89.

Paludi, M. A. (Ed.). (2008). *Understanding and preventing campus violence.* Westport, CT: Praeger.

Parcover, J. A., Dunton, E. C., Gehlert, K. M., & Mitchell, S. L. (2006). Getting the most from group counseling in college counseling centers. *Journal for Specialists in Group Work, 31,* 37–49.

Parish, K., & Friedman, J. C. (2011, February 7). Counselors, clients, and Facebook. *Counselor Magazine.* Retrieved April 12, 2011, from http://www.counselormagazine.com/feature-articles-mainmenu-63/61-professional-ethics/1149-counselors-clients-and-facebook

Parr, G. D., Jones, E. G., & Bradley, L. J. (2006). Facilitating effective committees. *Journal of Professional Counseling: Practice, Theory, and Research, 34,* 99–109.

Pate, R. H., Jr. (1995). Certification of specialties: Not if, but how. *Journal of Counseling and Development, 74,* 181–184.

Paterson, B., & Colbs, S. (2008). Navigating student privacy laws. *Leadership Exchange, 5,* 30–32. (Published by NASPA.)

Pavela, G. (2006). Should colleges withdraw students who threaten or attempt suicide? *Journal of American College Health, 54,* 367–371.

Pederson, P. B. (1991). Counseling international students. *The Counseling Psychologist, 19,* 10–58.

Perez, R. M., Fukuyama, M. A., & Coleman, N. C. (2005). Using the multicultural guidelines in college counseling centers. In M. G. Constantine & D. W. Sue (Eds.), *Strategies for building multicultural competence in mental health and educational settings* (pp. 160–179). Hoboken, NJ: John Wiley.

Petretic-Jackson, P., Pitman, L., & Jackson, T. (1996). Suicide postvention programs for university athletic departments. *Crisis Intervention and Time-Limited Treatment, 3,* 25–41.

Petry, N. M., Weinstock, J., Morasco, B. J., & Ledgerwood, D. M. (2009). Brief motivational interventions for college student problem gamblers. *Addiction, 104,* 1569–1578.

Phelps, R. E. (1992). University and college counseling centers: One option for new professionals in counseling psychology. *The Counseling Psychologist, 20,* 24–31.

Philip, A. F. (1990). Suicide and suicidal behavior: Postvention—counseling center response. *Journal of College Student Psychotherapy*, *4*, 195–209.

Phillips, L., Halstead, R., & Carpenter, W. (1996). The privatization of college counseling services: A preliminary investigation. *Journal of College Student Development*, *37*, 52–59.

Picca, L. H., & Feagin, J. R. (2007). *Two-faced racism: Whites in the backstage and frontstage*. New York: Routledge.

Pledge, D. S., Lapan, R. T., Heppner, P. P., Kivlighan, D., & Roehlke, H. J. (1998). Stability and severity of presenting problems at a university counseling center: A 6-year analysis. *Professional Psychology: Research and Practice*, *29*, 386–389.

Prescott, H. M. (2008). College mental health since the early twentieth century. *Harvard Review of Psychiatry*, *16*, 258–266.

Prieto, S. L. (1995). International student populations and needs assessment. In S. D. Stabb, S. M. Harris, & J. E. Talley (Eds.), *Multicultural needs assessment for college and university student populations* (pp. 203–223). Springfield, IL: Charles C Thomas.

Quintana, S. M., Yesenosky, J., Kilmartin, C., & Macias, D. (1991). Factors affecting referral decisions in a university counseling center. *Professional Psychology: Research and Practice*, *22*, 90–97.

Ramsay, J. R., & Rostain, A. L. (2006). Cognitive behavior therapy for college students with attention-deficit/hyperactivity disorder. *Journal of College Student Psychotherapy*, *21*, 3–20.

Rawls, D. T., Johnson, D., & Bartels, F. (2004). The counselor-in-residence program: Reconfiguring support services for a new millennium. *Journal of College Counseling*, *7*, 162–169.

Reilley, S. P. (2005). Empirically informed attention-deficit/hyperactivity disorder evaluation with college students. *Journal of College Counseling*, *8*, 153–164.

Reiss, B. (2011, January 30). Campus security and the specter of mental-health profiling. *The Chronicle of Higher Education*. Retrieved February 2, 2011, from http://chronicle.com/article/CampusSecuritythe/126075/?sid=& utm_source=at&utm_medium=en

Resnick, J. L. (2006). Strategies for implementation of the multicultural guidelines in university and college counseling centers. *Professional Psychology: Research and Practice*, *37*, 14–20.

Rettner, R. (2010, June 3). *Study: "Helicopter" parents make kids neurotic*. Retrieved June 4, 2010, from http://www.msnbc.msn.com/id/37493795/ns/health-kids_and_parenting/

Reynolds, A. L., & Pope, R. L. (2003). Multicultural competence in counseling centers. In D. B. Pope-Davis, H. L. Coleman, W. M. Liu, & R. L. Toporek (Eds.), *Handbook of multicultural competencies in counseling and psychology* (pp. 365–382). Thousand Oaks, CA: Sage.

Richards, M. M. (2009). Electronic medical records: Confidentiality issues in the time of HIPPA. *Professional Psychology: Research and Practice*, *40*, 550–556.

Richardson, M. S., & Massey, J. P. (1986). Counseling psychology training: Data and perceptions. *The Counseling Psychologist, 14*, 313–318.

Robbins, S. B., May, T. M., & Corazzini, J. G. (1985). Perceptions of client needs and counseling center staff roles and functions. *Journal of Counseling Psychology, 32*, 641–644.

Rockland-Miller, H. S., & Eells, G. T. (2006). The implementation of mental health clinical triage systems in university health services. *Journal of College Student Psychotherapy, 20*, 39–51.

Rodolfa, E. R. (1987). Training university faculty to assist emotionally troubled students. *Journal of College Student Personnel, 28*, 183–184.

Rodolfa, E. R., & Keilin, W. G. (2006). Internship training with licensure on the horizon. In T. J. Vaughn (Ed.), *Psychology licensure and certification: What students need to know* (pp. 73–83). Washington, DC: American Psychological Association.

Rollock, D. A., Westman, J. S., & Johnson, C. (1992). A Black student support group on a predominantly White university campus: Issues for counselors and therapists. *Journal for Specialists in Group Work, 17*, 243–252.

Ross, P. (1995). The stresses of directing a university counseling service. In W. Dryden (Ed.), *The stresses of counseling in action* (pp. 123–136). Thousand Oaks, CA: Sage.

Roth, S. G., Reed, R. A., & Donnelly, G. (2005). Building a campus crisis team. *International Journal of Emergency Mental Health, 7*, 307–314.

Roysircar, G., Sandhu, D. S., & Bibbins, V. E., Jr. (Eds.). (2003). *Multicultural competencies: A guidebook of practices.* Alexandria, VA: Association for Multicultural Counseling and Development.

Rudd, M. D. (2004). University counseling centers: Looking more and more like community clinics. *Professional Psychology: Research and Practice, 35*, 316–317.

Sack, R. T., Graham, M. F., & Simmons, K. P. (1995). Treatment groups for sexual abuse survivors on campus: Results of a national survey. *Journal of College Student Psychotherapy, 9*, 89–95.

Scanlon, C. R., & Gold, J. M. (1996). The balance between the missions of training and service at a university counseling center. *The Clinical Supervisor, 14*, 163–173.

Scholl, M. B., & Schmitt, D. M. (2009). Using motivational interviewing to address college client alcohol abuse. *Journal of College Counseling, 12*, 57–70.

Schreier, B. A. (1995). Moving beyond tolerance: A new paradigm for programming about homophobia/biphobia and heterosexism. *Journal of College Student Development, 36*, 19–26.

Schreier, B. A., & Bialk, S. E. (1997). Marketing an educational programming workshop series: An effective model and plan. *Journal of College Student Development, 38*, 89–91.

Schulte, B., & Jackman, T. (2009, August 20). Tech gunman's records reveal lack of treatment. *Washington Post.* Retrieved August 20, 2009, from http://www.washingtonpost.com/wp-dyn/content/article/2009/08/19/AR200908081902380.html

Schwartz, A. J. (2006). Are college students more disturbed today? Stability in the acuity and qualitative character of psychopathology of college counseling center clients: 1992–1993 through 2001–2002. *Journal of American College Health, 54,* 327–337.

Schwartz, A. J., & Whitaker, L. C. (1990). Suicide among college students: Assessment, treatment, and intervention. In S. J. Blumentahl & D. J. Kupfer (Eds.), *Suicide over the life cycle: Risk factors, assessment, and treatment of suicidal patients* (pp. 303–340). Washington, DC: American Psychiatric Press.

Schwartz, J. P., Griffin, L. D., Russell, M. M., & Frontaura-Duck, S. (2006). Prevention of dating violence on college campuses: An innovative program. *Journal of College Counseling, 9,* 90–96.

Schwartz, L. J., & Friedman, H. A. (2009). College student suicide. *Journal of College Student Psychotherapy, 23,* 78–102.

Schwitzer, A. M. (2003). A framework for college counseling responses to large scale traumatic incidents. *Journal of College Student Psychotherapy, 18,* 49–66.

Seamon, B. (2005). *Binge: What your college student won't tell you.* Hoboken, NJ: John Wiley.

Self, C. (2008). Advising delivery: Professional advisors, counselors, and other staff. In V. N. Gordon, W. R. Habley, & T. J. Grites (Eds.), *Academic advising: A comprehensive handbook* (2nd ed., pp. 267–278). San Francisco: Jossey-Bass.

Sesan, R. (1988–1989). Peer education: A creative resource for the eating disordered college student. *Journal of College Student Psychotherapy, 3,* 221–240.

Sharkin, B. S. (1995). Strains on confidentiality in college-student psychotherapy: Entangled therapeutic relationships, incidental encounters, and third-party inquiries. *Professional Psychology: Research and Practice, 26,* 184–189.

Sharkin, B. S. (1997). Increasing severity of presenting problems in college counseling centers: A closer look. *Journal of Counseling and Development, 75,* 275–281.

Sharkin, B. S. (2004a). Assessing changes in categories but not severity of counseling center client problems across 13 years: Comment on Benton, Robertson, Tseng, Newton, & Benton (2003). *Professional Psychology: Research and Practice, 35,* 313–315.

Sharkin, B. S. (2004b). College counseling and student retention: Research findings and implications for counseling centers. *Journal of College Counseling, 7,* 99–108.

Sharkin, B. S. (2006). *College students in distress: A resource guide for faculty, staff, and campus community.* Binghamton, NY: Haworth Press.

Sharkin, B. S. (2007). Against their will? Counseling mandated students. In J. A. Lippincott & R. B. Lippincott (Eds.), *Special populations in college counseling: A handbook for mental health professionals* (pp. 143–155). Alexandria, VA: American Counseling Association.

Sharkin, B. S., & Coulter, L. P. (2005). Empirically supporting the increasing severity of college counseling center client problems: Why is it so challenging? *Journal of College Counseling, 8,* 165–171.

Sharkin, B. S., & Coulter, L. P. (2009). Communication between college counselors and academic faculty when supervising graduate student trainees. *Journal of College Counseling, 12,* 162–169.

Sharkin, B. S., Scappaticci, A., & Birky, I. (1995). Access to confidential information in a university counseling center: A survey of referral sources. *Journal of College Student Development, 36,* 494–495.

Shea, R. H. (2002, February 18). On the edge on campus. *U.S. News and World Report, 132,* pp. 56–57.

Sheehy, J., & Commerford, M. (2006). Eating disorders. In P. A. Grayson & P. W. Meilman (Eds.), *College mental health practice* (pp. 261–280). New York: Brunner-Routledge.

Shuchman, M. (2007). Falling through the cracks: Virginia Tech and the restructuring of college mental health services. *The New England Journal of Medicine, 357,* 105–110.

Silverman, M. M. (2006). Suicide and suicidal behaviors. In P. A. Grayson & P. W. Meilman (Eds.), *College mental health practice* (pp. 303–323). New York: Brunner-Routledge.

Silverman, M. M., Meyer, P. M., Sloane, F., Raffel, M., & Pratt, D. M. (1997). The Big Ten student suicide study: A 10-year study of suicides on Midwestern university campuses. *Suicide and Life-Threatening Behavior, 27,* 285–303.

Singaravelu, H. D., & Pope, M. (Eds.). (2007). *A handbook for counseling international students in the United States.* Alexandria, VA: American Counseling Association.

Slimak, R. E., & Berkowitz, S. R. (1983). The university and college counseling center and malpractice suits. *The Personnel and Guidance Journal, 61,* 291–295.

Sloane, B. C., & Zimmer, C. G. (1993). The power of peer health education. *Journal of American College Health, 41,* 241–245.

Smith, K. L., & Rush, L. L. (2007). Counseling students who are deaf. In J. A. Lippincott & R. B. Lippincott (Eds.), *Special populations in college counseling: A handbook for mental health professionals* (pp. 231–245). Alexandria, VA: American Counseling Association.

Smith, R. B., & Fleming, D. L. (2007, April 20). Student suicide and colleges' liability. *The Chronicle of Higher Education, 53,* p. B24.

Smith, T. B., Dean, B., Floyd, S., Silva, C., Yamashita, M., Durtschi, J., & Heaps, R. A. (2007). Pressing issues in college counseling: A survey of American College Counseling Association members. *Journal of College Counseling, 10,* 64–78.

Snell, M. N., Mallinckrodt, B., Hill, R. D., & Lambert, M. J. (2001). Predicting counseling center clients' response to counseling: A 1-year follow-up. *Journal of Counseling Psychology, 48,* 463–473.

Spaulding, D. J., Eddy, J. P., & Chandras, K. V. (1997). Gulf War syndrome: Are campus health officials prepared to cope with Persian Gulf veterans? *College Student Journal, 31,* 317–322.

Steenbarger, B. N. (1998). Alcohol abuse and college counseling: An overview of research and practice. *Journal of College Counseling, 1,* 81–92.

Stone, G. L. (1993). Psychological challenges and responses to a campus tragedy: The Iowa experience. *Journal of College Student Psychotherapy, 8,* 259–271.

Stone, G. L., & Archer, J. A., Jr. (1990). College and university counseling centers in the 1990s: Challenges and limits. *The Counseling Psychologist, 18,* 539–607.

Stone, G. L., & Lucas, J. (1994). Disciplinary counseling in higher education: A neglected challenge. *Journal of Counseling and Development, 72,* 234–238.

Stone, G. L., Vespia, K. M., & Kanz, J. E. (2000). How good is mental health care on college campuses? *Journal of Counseling Psychology, 47,* 498–510.

Streufert, B. J. (2004). Death on campuses: Common postvention strategies in higher education. *Death Studies, 28,* 151–172.

Sturgeon, J. (2009, December 8). Suicide victim's parents sue Virginia Tech: Daniel Kim's estate says the university and its officials were negligent and seeks $43 million in damages. *The Roanoke Times.* Retrieved May 10, 2010, from http://www.roanoke.com/news/roanoke/wb/229037

Sue, D. W., Arredondo, P., & McDavis, R. J. (1992). Multicultural counseling competencies and standards: A call to the profession. *Journal of Counseling and Development, 70,* 477–486.

Sue, D. W., & Sue, D. (2003). *Counseling the culturally diverse: Theory and practice* (4th ed.). New York: Wiley.

Sulzberger, A. G., & Gabriel, T. (2011, January 13). College's policy on troubled students is under scrutiny. *New York Times.* Retrieved January 13, 2011, from http://www.nytimes.com/2011/01/14/us/14college.html?pagewanted=1&hp

Svanum, S., & Zody, Z. B. (2001). Psychopathology and college grades. *Journal of Counseling Psychology, 48,* 72–76.

Swenson, D. X., & Ginsberg, M. H. (1996). A comprehensive model for campus death postvention. *Journal of College Student Development, 37,* 543–549.

Tarvydas, V. M., & Hartley, M. T. (2009). What practitioners need to know about professional credentialing. In I. Marini & M. A. Stebnicki (Eds.), *The professional counselor's desk reference* (pp. 27–37). New York: Springer.

Terry, L. L. (1989). Assessing and constructing a meaningful system: Systemic perspective in a college counseling center. *Journal of Counseling and Development, 67,* 352–355.

Tryon, G. S. (1995). Issues to consider when instituting time limitations on individual counseling services. *Professional Psychology: Research and Practice, 26,* 620–623.

Turner, A. L., & Berry, T. R. (2000). Counseling center contributions to student retention and graduation: A longitudinal assessment. *Journal of College Student Development, 41,* 627–636.

Tyler, M. J., & Sabella, R. A. (2004). *Using technology to improve counseling practice: A primer for the 21st century.* Alexandria, VA: American Counseling Association.

Uffelman, R. A., & Hardin, S. I. (2002). Session limits at university counseling centers: Effects on help-seeking attitudes. *Journal of Counseling Psychology, 49,* 127–132.

Urbina, I. (2009, July 23). Va. Tech gunman's mental health records found. *New York Times.* Retrieved July 23, 2009, from http://www.nytimes.com/2009/07/23/us/23vtech.html?_r=1&pagewanted=print

Utterback, J., & Caldwell, J. (1989). Proactive and reactive approaches to PTSD in the aftermath of campus violence: Forming a traumatic stress react team. *Journal of Traumatic Stress, 2,* 171–183.

Vespia, K. M. (2007). A national survey of small college counseling centers: Successes, issues, and challenges. *Journal of College Student Psychotherapy, 22,* 17–40.

Vinson, M. L. (1995). Employing family therapy in group counseling with college students: Similarities and a technique employed in both. *Journal for Specialists in Group Work, 20,* 240–252.

Virginia Tech Review Panel. (2007). *Mass shootings at Virginia Tech, April 16, 2007.* Retrieved March 10, 2010, from http://www.vtreviewpanel.org/report/index.html

Vogel, S. A., Leyser, Y., Wyland, S., & Brulle, A. (1999). Students with learning disabilities in higher education: Faculty attitudes and practices. *Learning Disabilities Research and Practice, 14,* 173–186.

Von Steen, P. G. (2000). Traditional-age college students. In D. C. Davis & K. M. Humphrey (Eds.), *College counseling: Issues and strategies for a new millennium* (pp. 111–131). Alexandria, VA: American Counseling Association.

Wachowiak, D. G., & Simono, R. B. (1996). Psychologists in counseling centers: Fifteen years later. *The Counseling Psychologist, 24,* 498–507.

Waldo, M. (1989). Primary prevention in university residence halls: Paraprofessional-led relationship enhancement groups for college roommates. *Journal of Counseling and Development, 67,* 465–471.

Walker, L. A., & Conyne, R. K. (2007). Group work with international students. In H. D. Singaravelu & M. Pope (Eds.), *A handbook for counseling international students in the United States* (pp. 299–309). Alexandria, VA: American Counseling Association.

Wasley, P. (2007, February 9). A secret support network: Behind the scenes, Hanover College's "early alert team" tries to help students stay on course. *The Chronicle of Higher Education, 53,* p. A27.

Weissberg, M. (1987). Testing services in college and university counseling centers. *Journal of Counseling and Development, 65,* 253–256.

Welch, P. J. (1996). In search of a caring community: Group therapy for gay, lesbian and bisexual college students. *Journal of College Student Psychotherapy, 11*, 27–40.

Welkowitz, L. A., & Baker, L. J. (2005). Supporting college students with Asperger's syndrome. In L. J. Baker & L. A. Welkowitz (Eds.), *Asperger's syndrome: Intervening in schools, clinics, and communities* (pp. 173–187). Mahwah, NJ: Lawrence Erlbaum.

Wertheim, L. J. (2010, May 17). Did Yeardley Love have to die? *Sports Illustrated, 112*, 28–34.

Westefeld, J. S., Homaifar, B., Spotts, J., Furr, S., Range, L., & Werth, J. L. (2005). Perceptions concerning college student suicide: Data from four universities. *Suicide and Life-Threatening Behavior, 35*, 640–645.

Westefeld, J. S., Maples, M. R., Buford, B., & Taylor, S. (2001). Gay, lesbian, and bisexual college students: The relationship between sexual orientation and depression, loneliness, and suicide. *Journal of College Student Psychotherapy, 15*, 71–82.

Westefeld, J. S., Whitchard, K. A., & Range, L. M. (1990). College and university student suicide: Trends and implications. *The Counseling Psychologist, 18*, 464–476.

Whitaker, L. C. (1992). Prescription psychotropic drugs and psychotherapy: Adjunctive or disjunctive? *Journal of College Student Psychotherapy, 7*, 79–92.

Whitaker, L. C. (2006). Relationships. In P. A. Grayson & P. W. Meilman (Eds.), *College mental health practice* (pp. 95–112). New York: Brunner-Routledge.

Whitaker, L. C. (2007). Forces pushing prescription psychotropic drugs in college mental health. *Journal of College Student Psychotherapy, 21*, 1–25.

White, V. E., Trepal, H., Petuch, A., & Ilko Hancock, S. (2007). Self-injurious behavior: Counseling students who self-injure. In J. A. Lippincott & R. B. Lippincott (Eds.), *Special populations in college counseling: A handbook for mental health professionals* (pp. 297–308). Alexandria, VA: American Counseling Association.

Widseth, J. C., Webb, R. E., & John, K. B. (1997). The question of outsourcing: The role and functions of college counseling services. *Journal of College Student Psychotherapy, 11*, 3–22.

Wiesen, E. F., & Lischer, D. K. (2006). College crisis intervention: An initiative to develop regional campus critical incident stress management teams. *International Journal of Emergency Mental Health, 8*, 183–187.

Wilczenski, F. L. (1992). Coming to terms with an identity of "learning disabled" in college. *Journal of College Student Psychotherapy, 7*, 49–61.

Williams, E. N., & Edwardson, T. L. (2000). Managed care and counseling centers: Training issues for the new millennium. *Journal of College Student Psychotherapy, 14*, 51–65.

Winerip, M. (2011, January 24). Positives with roots in tragedy on campus. *New York Times.* Retrieved February 10, 2011, from http://www.nytimes.com/2011/01/24/education/24winerip.html

Witchel, R. I. (1991). The impact of dysfunctional families on college students' development. *New Directions for Student Services, 54*, 5–17.

Wlazelek, B., & Coulter, L. P. (1999). The role of counseling services for students in academic jeopardy: A preliminary study. *Journal of College Counseling, 2*, 33–41.

Wlazelek, B., & Hartman, K. (2007). Counseling for success: Assisting students in academic jeopardy. In J. A. Lippincott & R. B. Lippincott (Eds.), *Special populations in college counseling: A handbook for mental health professionals* (pp. 173–185). Alexandria, VA: American Counseling Association.

Wolgast, B. M., Lambert, M. J., & Puschner, B. (2003). The dose-response relationship at a college counseling center: Implications for setting session limits. *Journal of College Student Psychotherapy, 18*, 15–29.

Wolgast, B. M., Rader, J., Roche, D., Thompson, C. P., von Zuben, F. C., & Goldberg, A. (2005). Investigation of clinically significant change by severity level in college counseling center clients. *Journal of College Counseling, 8*, 140–152.

Wood, C. (2005). Supervisory working alliance: A model providing direction for college counseling supervision. *Journal of College Counseling, 8*, 127–137.

Wright, D. J. (1999). Group services for students of color. In Y. Jenkins (Ed.), *Diversity in college settings: Directions for helping professionals* (pp. 149–167). Florence, KY: Taylor & Francis/Routledge.

Wright, D. J. (2000). College counseling and the needs of multicultural students. In D. C. Davis & K. M. Humphrey (Eds.), *College counseling: Issues and strategies for a new millennium* (pp. 153–168). Alexandria, VA: American Counseling Association.

Yakushko, O., Davidson, M. M., & Sanford-Martens, T. C. (2008). Seeking help in a foreign land: International students' use patterns for a U.S. university counseling center. *Journal of College Counseling, 11*, 6–18.

Yau, T. Y. (2004). Guidelines for facilitating groups with international college students. In J. L. DeLucia-Waack, D. A. Gerrity, C. Kalodner, & M. T. Riva (Eds.), *Handbook of group counseling and psychotherapy* (pp. 366–377). Thousand Oaks, CA: Sage.

Yorgason, J. B., Linville, D., & Zitzman, B. (2008). Mental health among college students: Do those who need services know about and use them? *Journal of American College Health, 57*, 173–181.

Yost, P. (2010, April 16). *Government report sees increase in campus violence.* Retrieved April 17, 2010, from http://www.huffingtonpost.com/2010/04/16/govt-report-sees-increase_n_540699.html

Young, J. R. (2003, February 14). Prozac campus: More students seek counseling and take psychiatric medication. *The Chronicle of Higher Education, 49*, pp. A37–A38.

Zubernis, L., & Snyder, M. (2007). Considerations of additional stressors and developmental issues for gay, lesbian, bisexual, and transgender college students. *Journal of College Student Psychotherapy, 22*, 75–79.

Zunker, V. G. (2008). *Career, work, and mental health: Integrating career and personal counseling.* Thousand Oaks, CA: Sage.

Index

A

ACA. *see* American Counseling Association (ACA)
Academic advising, 51–52
Academic affairs, counseling centers and, 99
Academic counseling, 24–26
Academic difficulties, 18
Academic failure, 25
ACCA. *see* American College Counseling Association (ACCA)
Accreditation of Counseling and Related Educational Programs, 11
ACHA. *see* American College Health Association (ACHA)
Addiction counseling, 23–24, 77
ADHD. *see* Attention-deficit/ hyperactivity disorder (ADHD)
Adjunct instructor, serving as, 68

Administrative duties, 48–49, 119
Administrators, college counselors and, 98–100
Adult college students, 86
Adult learners, 86
Affsprung, E. H., 103
After-hours emergencies, crisis intervention and, 29, 32–34
Alcohol use/abuse, 13, 22, 23, 64, 116
Allies (for GLBTQ students and those who support GLBTQ students), 91
Amada, G., 7, 97
American Board of Professional Psychology, 76
American College Counseling Association (ACCA), 74–75
American College Counseling Association's Community College Task Force, 119

community colleges and, 118–119

crisis intervention and emergency coverage, 28–35

during economic turmoil, 124

fees and, 123, 124, 126–127

merging with health services, 130–131

outreach programming and, 89

research and, 71

student affairs and, 98

Counselor-in-residence program, 41

Couples counseling, 21

Crime Awareness and Campus Security Act of 1990. *see* Jeanne Clery Disclosure of Campus Security Policy and Crime Statistics Act

Crisis events, 65–66

Crisis intervention, 28–35, 125

Crisis response, college counselors and, 57–59, 65–66

Crisis Response Team (CRT), 65–66

Crisis situation response titles, 58

Criteria for counseling, 17-18

Critical Incident Management, 58

CRT. *see* Crisis Response Team (CRT)

Cyberbullying, 63

Cyberstalking, 63

D

Data collection, counseling centers and, 73

Dating and relationships, 40

Davenport, R., 106

Davis, J. M., 34

Dean, L. A., 119

Death

of family member, 29

of staff and faculty members, 34–35

Delgado-Romero, E. A., 84

Demand, individual counseling and, 19

Department of Education, on violence on and off campus, 62–63

Department of Education's Office for Civil Rights, 63

Depression, 18, 24, 40

Developmental problems, counseling and, 18

Diagnostic and Statistical Manual of Mental Disorders, 4th ed. (*DSM-IV-TR;* American Psychiatric Association, 2000), 13

Diversified interest clubs, 91

Diversity

college counseling and incorporating, 83–84

embracing, 82–83

introduction to, 81

meeting students needs on campus, 84–91

university committees and, 67

Diversity-sensitive counseling, provision of, 87–88

Doctoral degree *vs.* degree, college counselor and, 11

Doctoral-level clinicians, in college counseling centers, 11

Doctoral-level practitioners, in college counseling centers, 10–11

Documentation, 49

Dominican Student Association, 91

Dual/multiple role relationships, 102

Duffey, T., 40